❋ Middletown Jews ❋

Middletown Jews

The Tenuous Survival of an American Jewish Community

EDITED BY
DAN ROTTENBERG

WITH AN INTRODUCTION BY
DWIGHT W. HOOVER

Indiana University Press
Bloomington and Indianapolis

Publication of this book is made possible in part with the assistance of a Challenge Grant from the National Endowment for the Humanities, a federal agency that supports research, education, and public programming in the humanities.

This book is a publication of

Indiana University Press
601 North Morton Street
Bloomington, IN 47404-3797 USA

http://www.indiana.edu/~iupress

Telephone orders 800-842-6796
Fax orders 812-855-7931
Orders by email iuporder@indiana.edu

The paper used in this publication meets the minimum requirements of American National Standard for Information Sciences—Permanence of Paper for Printed Library Materials, ANSI Z39.48-1984.

Manufactured in the United States of America

Library of Congress Cataloging-in-Publication Data

Middletown Jews : the tenuous survival of an American Jewish community / edited by Dan Rottenberg ; with an introduction by Dwight M. Hoover.
    p.   cm.
Includes bibliographical references.
ISBN 0-253-33243-5 (cloth : alk. paper)
1. Jews—Indiana—Muncie—History.   2. Jews—Indiana—Muncie —Biography.   3. Muncie (Ind.)—Ethnic relations.   4. Muncie (Ind.)—Biography.
5. Oral history. I. Rottenberg, Dan.
F534.M9M53   1997
977.2'65—dc20 96-2279

ISBN 0-253-21206-5 (pbk. : alk. paper)

2 3 4 5 6 02 01 00 99 98

CONTENTS

PREFACE
BEYOND THE LOWER EAST SIDE

In the early 1920s the sociologists Robert and Helen Lynd undertook a uniquely ambitious project: They set out to study the life of a typical American community in much the same detached manner that anthropologists examine the life of Australian aborigines. They would find a city that was "as representative as possible of contemporary American life" and place the entire community under the microscope of social science.

The two books that subsequently emerged from the Lynds' research—*Middletown* in 1929 and *Middletown in Transition* in 1937—described in detail an anonymous self-contained city of more than 35,000 population somewhere in the Midwest. Within the nearly 1,200 pages of these two books, virtually nothing about this typically American town escaped the Lynds' notice—including, here and there, references to a minuscule and equally anonymous Jewish community.

"The Jewish population of Middletown," the Lynds wrote in *Middletown in Transition*, "is so small as to be numerically negligible. . . . Jews in Middletown are quietly on the defensive. . . . There is frank discrimination at critical points such as membership in Rotary, but in general it is mild, and the facts that the Jewish group is so small, is made up of small merchants, and does not force the issue on the city make the Jewish issue slight." However, the Lynds added, "the issue is tinder ready for kindling if and as Middletown wants a bonfire to burn a scapegoat."

The tinder had already been kindled between 1923 and 1925, when the Ku Klux Klan dominated Middletown's politics. Klan torchlight parades often marched through the downtown streets, passing many shops that were operated by Middletown's Jewish merchants. African Americans and Catholics were the primary targets of Klan hatred; Jews came next. "We are charged with being against the Jew," thundered a lawyer from the state capital at a Klan rally reported by the Lynds. "We are against no man. Jesus Christ is the leader of the Ku Klux Klan, and we are for Him. The Jew is not for Him, and therefore the Jew has shut himself out of the Klan." Of course, Indiana was not the only northern state in which the Klan possessed strength. Wisconsin, Pennsylvania, and even Oregon—to name a few—had large Klan movements. And, regrettably, anti-Semitism would have existed in America even if the Klan had never existed.

Because they were vastly outnumbered—there were never more than two hundred of them at any given time—for many years the Jews of Middletown tended to swallow this animosity in silence. These reticent Jews seemed to bear no resemblance to the boisterous immigrant masses of New York's Lower East Side or South Philadelphia or Chicago's Maxwell Street. Nor did they resemble the confident financiers of America's nineteenth-century German-Jewish business elite or the proud standard-bearers of America's eighteenth-century Sephardic-Jewish aristocracy. The Jews of Middletown spent their lives isolated from the mainstream of Jewish life even as they functioned daily amid the mainstream of American life.

In the best objective tradition of social science, the Lynds never publicly identified their generic "Middletown," nor did they identify by name the businesses, organizations, schools, colleges, and people they discussed in their pages. But of course the pseudonymous Middletown was in fact the real city of Muncie, Indiana, and the faceless Middletown Jews alluded to by the Lynds were real people as well.

Whether Muncie was or is a "typical" American community is, of course, a matter of subjective judgment. But to the extent that it has been typically American, it has also been *atypically* Jewish. Through most of the twentieth century, Jews have comprised roughly 2.5 to 3 percent of the U.S. population, and much larger proportions in the cities where they tended to cluster; but in Muncie the Jews have never accounted for more than a fraction of a percentage point. And whereas in 1984 Illinois had a Jewish population of 260,000, or 2.5 percent of the state's population, and Ohio had 140,000 Jews (1.3%), and Michigan counted 85,000 (1%), Indiana in that same year had a Jewish population of only 21,000, or four-tenths of one percent of the state's total.[1] Moreover, this statewide figure actually represented a decline since the turn of the twentieth century, when Indiana's Jewish population was estimated at 25,000.[2]

These statistics reflect more than mere numbers, for the role of the community is central in Jewish life. A Jew senses it instinctively, in synagogue, in *shiva* following a death, in the injunction to assemble a *minyan*—that is, at least ten people—in order to pray, in the recognition that expulsion from the community is Judaism's gravest penalty. Without a critical mass of numbers a Jewish community—and thus the viability of Jewish consciousness—is vulnerable to extinction. The result is a community whose outlook, as the Lynds astutely noted, tends to be perpetually defensive.

Long after the Klan had faded from public life in Indiana, anti-Semitism continued. In Muncie, as elsewhere, through the 1950s, Jews were prevented from living in certain parts of town, excluded from business and professional clubs, and barred from the city's only country club. At first glance, the Jews of medium-sized cities like Muncie seem to have suffered the worst of all possible bargains: Muncie's Jewish community was large enough to provoke anti-Semitic restrictions but too small to support a full-time rabbi, a YMHA, a Jewish center, cultural organizations, or anything more than the barest sense of communal identity.

Muncie's Temple Beth El Congregation, founded in the late 1870s, remained small throughout its history and rarely had funds to engage a full-time rabbi, relying instead on part-time rabbinical students at Hebrew Union College in Cincinnati, 120 miles south. The varied religious backgrounds of the temple's members—Reform, Orthodox, free-thinkers—led to conflicting visions of the temple's mission: Was it primarily needed for Sabbath services, for Sunday School, for High Holidays, or for social functions? Yet even a Jew who completely abandoned his religion could never be fully accepted in a city which believed, as the Lynds put it, "that individual Jews may be all right but that as a race one doesn't care to mix too much with them."

What sort of Jew would settle in such a place? How could a Jewish identity survive here? Could such an experience produce anything of value to Judaism?

In 1850 a newspaper called *The Muncietonian* carried an advertisement for L. and H. Marks and Company, a dry goods and clothing store owned by the brothers Lipman and Henry Marks—the first evidence of a Jewish presence in an unincorporated frontier town of 600 people—a town that had first been settled in 1820 and that, until 1852, lacked even a railroad connection to the outside world.

Over the next century and even to the present day, most of Muncie's non-Jewish arrivals came from nearby farms and villages; for them, Muncie was a way-station on the road to a larger metropolis. But Muncie's Jewish arrivals followed a different pattern: Most of them came from larger and more sophisticated cities, like Indianapolis, Chicago, Cincinnati, Cleveland, New Orleans, Natchez, Flint. They belonged as well to the small minority of immigrants—especially small among Jewish immigrants—who perceived and seized economic opportunities in the small towns and rural areas of America's heartland and moved there despite the virtual absence of Jewish community life. Both their Jewishness and their urban backgrounds set them apart within Muncie, and their distance from the big cities simultaneously isolated them from mainstream American Jewish life.

By the mid-twentieth century the Jews of Muncie had expanded from retail clothing stores and scrap metal yards into such fields as law, optometry, liquor, jewelry, wholesale paper distribution, linen service, hotel management, real estate, and finance companies. Their attraction to retailing slowed and ultimately halted with the advent, in the 1950s, of competition from chain stores and from suburban malls in larger cities made suddenly accessible on interstate highways.

Of the Jewish-owned stores which had once dominated Muncie's Walnut Street shopping district, only one remained by 1979. By that time, as well, virtually all anti-Jewish restrictions had been removed from Muncie's housing, civic organizations, and country clubs. Yet Muncie's Jewish community again seemed threatened with extinction—not by hostility this time, but simply by the geographic mobility and transience of American life in general. A new generation of Munsonians— Jews and gentiles alike—was growing up blissfully unaware of the bigotry of the Ku Klux Klan years and the genteel prejudice of the '30s and '40s.

In that year, a lifelong Jewish resident of Muncie named Martin Schwartz—owner of a local paper distribution company, Harvard graduate, and amateur historian—grew concerned that his generation's collective experiences would soon be lost to posterity. To avoid that fate, he commissioned two professors at Ball State University to interview the older members of Muncie's Jewish community—some two dozen men and women who had survived the turbulent '20s and '30s as children or adults and had helped engineer the subsequent acceptance of Muncie Jews by the larger gentile community.

In effect this project removed the mask of anonymity that had long concealed the faceless Jews of Middletown and enabled them to step forward for the first time as the flesh-and-blood individual Jews of Muncie, Indiana. In the process of recording their individual stories, these isolated American Jews made an odd discovery about themselves: Without anyone's consciously realizing it, they had collectively sculpted their own unique and valuable identity out of their adversity.

Irving Howe, author of *World of Our Fathers*, once remarked that nothing of consequence to the American Jewish experience had occurred outside the major urban centers like New York, Philadelphia, and Chicago. But as Dwight Hoover, one of the Muncie project's two interviewers, observed at the time: "One thread runs through all the transcripts: a commitment to life regardless of the odds, a courage that enabled its possessors to persevere in times of difficulty and without much support, and a zest to continue life even though that life had not been easy. If these qualities can be summed up in one word, that word would be *indomitable*. I can think of no greater heritage than that and no element of character more needed today."

As a gentile idealizing his Jewish subjects, Hoover can be forgiven for overstating his point. The word that most of Muncie's Jews themselves would choose to characterize their community, past and present, is not *indomitable* but *vulnerable*. That community may very well vanish from Muncie in the next generation, just as countless small Jewish communities across America have vanished in the second half of the twentieth century. But the Jews of Muncie have indeed contributed something important to American Jewish life: a demonstration that Jewish individuals armed with the slenderest human and financial resources can create and sustain a viable Jewish community as they feel the need to do so.

DAN ROTTENBERG
PHILADELPHIA

NOTES

1. Jacob Rader Marcus, *To Count a People: Jewish Population Data* (1990).
2. See article on Indiana in the *Jewish Encyclopedia*, Funk, 1901–06.

EDITOR'S NOTE

The nineteen interviews excerpted here were conducted in 1979 by C. Warren Vander Hill and Dwight W. Hoover, professors at Ball State University. The original transcripts of those interviews are available at the Center for Middletown Studies in the Bracken Library at Ball State University in Muncie, Indiana. For purposes of this book, the interviews have been edited for clarity, readability, and avoidance of redundancy. Supplemental observations by the editor are cited in brackets or footnotes.

The book's introduction by Dwight W. Hoover, "To Be a Jew in Middletown: A Muncie Oral History Project," originally appeared in the *Indiana Magazine of History*, Vol. LXXI (June 1985). That version is essentially unchanged here except for the updating of information and some factual corrections.

■

About the Illustrations

The task of rescuing images for posterity may be even more challenging than preserving memories. Old photos can lead a precarious existence, often tossed out at the whim of an overwhelmed heir and lost forever. The act of reproducing old family photographs here not only enhances this book but assists Martin Schwartz's goal of preserving Muncie's Jewish community for posterity. I am grateful to Bernard Freund, Flo Lapin, Herb Pazol, Joe Freadlin, Bud Roth, Pearl Shonfield, and especially Martin D. Schwartz for providing these glimpses into the past. Marty Schwartz not only loaned us some of his own treasured family photos and had others reproduced from the collection of the Ball State University Center for Middletown Studies but also persistently cajoled and collected pictures from other interviewees and their descendants—a process that consumed considerably more time than he anticipated when he first volunteered for it.

D.R.

INTRODUCTION

TO BE A JEW IN MIDDLETOWN

DWIGHT W. HOOVER

Middletown: A Study in Contemporary American Culture (1929), the famous study of Muncie, Indiana, by Robert S. and Helen Merrell Lynd, says very little about the town's small Jewish community. Indeed, the only specific indication that such a community even existed comes as a kind of footnote to the prevailing Protestantism in Muncie. The Lynds mention that the Jewish merchants whose stores lined Walnut Street, the major thoroughfare, faced a dilemma because the biggest shopping day of the week was Saturday, the Jewish Sabbath, and retail stores generally closed on Sunday. The Lynds then note that there was no uniform Jewish solution to this dilemma; many owners opened on Saturday, a few closed their stores on Friday afternoon for the entire weekend.

The failure to study the Jewish community is not surprising given (1) the intent of the sponsors of the Lynds' work, the Institute of Social and Religious Research; (2) the criteria used for selecting a town to survey; and (3) the Lynds' assumptions about the nature of both American religion and society. The Institute of Social and Religious Research planned to survey an entire community's religious practices, with the long-term goal of uniting all Protestant churches in the country.[1] In choosing Muncie, Robert S. Lynd used criteria that specifically de-emphasized heterogeneity, revealing his interest in analyzing only older stock American Protestants. One such criterion was that the city to be studied have only a small proportion of "negro [*sic*] and foreign-born population."[2] Further, although Lynd was himself a graduate of Union Theological Seminary, he viewed traditional religion as a relic of pre-industrial society, doomed to die as society modernized. He did not regard religion as significant in itself but conceived of it as a refuge for workers from the pressures of an industrial system.[3] Finally, to compound the problem, Lynd's model of society was almost exclusively an industrial one that slighted small retail businesses to concentrate upon large manufacturing establishments, thus overlooking that segment of the town's economy by which a majority of Muncie's Jews made a living. All of these factors contributed to the minimal coverage of Jews in *Middletown*.

An opportunity to remedy this oversight came in 1979 when a local businessman, Martin D. Schwartz, commissioned Ball State University professors Warren Vander Hill and Dwight W. Hoover to begin an oral history of Muncie's Jewish community. Schwartz was anxious to record the memories of the older members of the community since he feared these might soon be lost (a fear which was justified, as nine of the interviewees have since died). Nineteen persons, ranging in age from sixty to ninety-three, were interviewed. The interviewers used as a guide a questionnaire devised by the Indiana Jewish Historical Society, which was modified to include more questions on social and physical mobility and family relationships. The intent was not merely to record disparate memories of individuals and their families but to find a coherent pattern, if one existed, in the total group experience. The next step was to compare this experience with that of other groups in other cities and to compare the attitudes of Jewish citizens of Muncie with those explored by the Lynds in their classic work. In order to accomplish all these goals, it was necessary to re-interview some persons and to obtain data from printed sources, such as city directories and county histories, to supplement the information originally obtained.[4]

The most striking quality of Muncie's Jewish population was its restlessness, as individuals moved in and out of town searching for greater economic opportunity. The attraction to Muncie was usually the offer of a partnership in a scrap business or a job clerking in a clothing store; the person making the offer was often a relative, either by blood or by marriage. But the attraction was not strong enough to ensure permanent residence; the migrant often moved out again. If successful as a partner or clerk, the recently arrived migrant might open his business in another, larger city. If unsuccessful, he might seek a more promising future elsewhere. City directories and cemetery records provide evidence of this mobility. The restless movement from town to town in the nineteenth century certainly paralleled that of the typical urban migrant who, according to Stephan Thernstrom, "moved through three or more communities before he settled down around middle age."[5]

Although individuals came and went, businesses often remained. An entrepreneur would come to Muncie, often from a larger city such as Cincinnati with a significant Jewish population, and establish a business. That person would then employ other members of the family who would help expand the store. The original owner might sell the store to one of these persons and move on. The name would change, reflecting the new owner, but the business would not.

This pattern of movement applied to Jewish migrants generally, regardless of national origin. While most of the early migrants to Muncie were from Western Europe, the first citizens had similar experiences and followed similar behavior patterns to those of later arrivals who were from Eastern Europe or who had been born in the United States. All worked within a narrow range of occupations and apparently moved easily in the town with little sense of discrimination, joining in the activities of the larger community.

A few examples help illustrate the beginnings of the Jewish community. The first Jewish settlers in Muncie, according to Alexander L. Shonfield, were Henry and Lipman Marks, who had opened a dry goods and clothing store by 1850, four years before the incorporation of the town.[6] Natives of Alsace, the Markses had immigrated to the United States in the 1840s. The Markses brought four relatives to Muncie to work in the store; these six persons constituted almost 25 percent of the foreign-born population of Muncie, thus making French-born residents the third most numerous immigrant group after the Irish and the Germans.[7] But the Markses did not remain in Muncie long. They soon moved to Cincinnati, where prospects seemed brighter; however, the store remained.

A somewhat later arrival, Frank Leon, duplicated the Markses' success in the clothing business in Muncie and Cincinnati, the former town serving as his home base. Leon had a retail store in Muncie but later expanded into clothing manufacturing in Cincinnati, supplying his retail store and others with his own products. Leon was the most spectacular example of Jewish integration into the life of the community in the nineteenth century. Among the civic groups he was instrumental in founding were the Knights of Pythias, the Muncie Choral Society, the Citizens' Enterprise Company (a forerunner of the Commercial Club and the Chamber of Commerce, designed to promote industrial and commercial development of the city), and, most remarkably, the Home Missionary Society (an organization formed to offer charitable relief and Christian education).[8]

By the 1870s, Jews from areas other than France began to arrive. The first was Lee Dessaur, who was American born and who came to Muncie from Cincinnati in order to marry the daughter of a retail clothier. Dessaur, however, did not follow in his father-in-law's footsteps by taking over the store. Instead he became a wholesale liquor dealer, the first Jewish entrepreneur not in the clothing business in Muncie.[9] In that same decade came the first Jew from Eastern Europe. He was Polish-born Heiman Silverburg, who had lived in Natchez,

Mississippi, for twenty-two years prior to moving with his family to Muncie to open a merchant tailoring business.[10] Both Dessaur and Silverburg signaled the expansion of vocational opportunity and the growing heterogeneity of Muncie's Jewish community.

By the 1880s other Eastern European Jews had joined Silverburg as the mass immigration from Eastern Europe began. The first to arrive was the Cohen family. The father, Moses Cohen, had migrated from Poland to Indianapolis in 1874. There he married Sarah Ringolsky, the daughter of Herschel Ringolsky (later changed to Ringold), who had also migrated from Poland.[11] After living in Indianapolis for a time, the Cohens moved to Muncie. They were pioneers in the scrap business, becoming the first Jews in that trade. Their business was quite successful; both it and the Cohen family grew. After twenty-six years in Muncie, the family moved to Chicago to exploit the success of the older sons in the scrap business there, retaining ownership on a building in Muncie. Just after World War I a daughter, Pearl, moved back with her husband, Will Freund, to open a clothing store in the Cohen Building.[12]

This progression was duplicated, only much more rapidly, by the Ringolds, the second Polish-born Jewish family to arrive in Muncie in the 1880s. Herschel Ringold joined his son-in-law Moses Cohen in the scrap business a year after Moses opened his yard, but he left part of his family in Indianapolis. Herschel's son Samuel subsequently came to Muncie to enter the clothing business.

Two other families of Eastern European origin showed a willingness—typical of American society in general—to venture into different enterprises even in a community where their families were established in others. The Schwartzes and the Feinbergs both came to Muncie in the last decade of the nineteenth century. The first Schwartz to arrive was one of three brothers. A native of Lithuania, Samuel Schwartz peddled shoestrings and shoelaces, then clerked in a shoe store before open-

ing the Economy Shoe Store in Muncie. His brother Maurice
arrived in town about the same time to work as a salesman
in a clothing store. While Samuel settled permanently in
Muncie, Maurice did not. He went to the Yukon during the
Klondike gold rush, among other things, and then returned
to Matthews, Indiana, to take advantage of the gas boom by
manufacturing glass chimneys for kerosene lamps. While
there he employed the third Schwartz brother, Leo, to sell
the glass chimneys. When the gas supply dwindled and electricity arrived, Maurice returned to Muncie to open the Moxie
Clothing Store, which specialized in expensive men's
clothes. Leo worked as a traveling salesman for paper companies until 1920, when he too came to Muncie to open a
wholesale paper supply company. Here he remained until
his death. But Maurice, ever restless, left in the late 1920s
for New York City, where he again changed occupations and
went into the dry-cleaning business.[13]

Another Polish-born migrant in the 1890s reversed the common tendency to change from scrap dealer to clothing store
owner. Abraham Feinberg moved to Muncie from Columbus,
Indiana, in 1898. After selling clothes for two years, he went
into the scrap business, which he used as a stepping stone to a
manufacturing career. He eventually owned Muncie Cap and
Set Screw Company and was reputed to be the richest Jew in
Muncie.[14]

The history of Jewish migration and occupational choice in
Muncie, while similar in some ways to the experience of other
cities, is also different. On the one hand, Jewish migration to
Muncie appears to resemble migration elsewhere in America,
as described by William Toll:

> In America . . . the migrants provided the shelters and
> jobs for relatives, especially brothers and nephews, and
> in the towns of the Midwest and West seem easily to have
> entered social and political elites. As Robert E. Levinson
> has shown for individual Jews in the California gold rush

towns, and as Steven Hertzberg has more carefully ana-
lyzed in his pathbreaking study of Atlanta Jewry, the
young peddlers were accustomed to continual migration
through family sponsorship. Nevertheless, their persis-
tence rates in specific towns were high compared with
gentiles, in some cases even when compared with gentile merchants.[15]

On the other hand, the occupational choices of Muncie's
Jews seem more diverse and less predictable than those in other,
larger communities. In other cities there appears to have been
greater continuity between occupations in Europe and America
as well as continuity in clientele for those who were peddlers.
Marc Lee Raphael, for example, has found that Jews from Eastern Europe who migrated to Columbus, Ohio, because the factory system had undercut their work as peddlers, continued
to perform the same type of work in Columbus as they had in
the Old World.[16] Jews in Steelton, Pennsylvania, who had been
peddlers in Russia and Poland, moved from peddling to the
retail trade. By 1940 they constituted over half the shopkeepers in Steelton; however, the kind of customers in these Jewish-owned shops had not changed. They consisted of the in-
dustrializing peasants from Eastern and Central Europe and
southern Italy.[17] In Europe these people had been served in
little agricultural villages; in America they were served in industrial towns. Thus Polish-born Jews sold work clothing to
Polish-born laborers in the Old World and the New. These
trends are less evident in Muncie, however, where there were
few Polish immigrants to cater to.

In order to demonstrate this point, it is useful to reconstruct
the structure of the Jewish-owned businesses in Muncie in the
heyday of the 1920s and then to consider the variety of stores
and the background of the owners. These stores mainly lined
Walnut Street, the major shopping street in the town, with the
lower-numbered stores being in a more fashionable area and
the higher numbers in a poorer, transitional one.

Sam Ringold's Clothing Store	109 South Walnut
The Why (Will Freund)	525 South Walnut
Economy Shoe Store (Samuel Schwartz)	116 North Walnut
The Moxie Company (Maurice Schwartz)	200 block of South Walnut
Schwartz Paper Company (Leo Schwartz)	628 South Walnut
Marx and Kallmeyer Clothing Store	104–106 North Walnut
(Herman Marx and David Kallmeyer)	
Charles Indorf's Pawn Shop	608–612 South Walnut
King's Clothing Shop (Charles Indorf)	125 South Walnut
Pazol's Jewelry Store (Harry D. Pazol)	206 South Walnut
Victor Garment Company	424 South Walnut
(Morris Shapiro)	
Muncie Typewriter Exchange	220 North Walnut
(Jack D. Burgauer)	
Sam Gold's Clothing Store	512 South Walnut
New York Hat Company (Joseph Levy)	109 North Walnut
Moses Hene's Clothing Store	120 South Walnut
Herman Eichel's Millinery Shop	309 South Walnut
Louis Friedman's Pipe Supplies	520 Wysor Street
Alexander Shonfield's Clothing Store	112 South Walnut
Roberts Hotel (George Roberts)	424 South High
Klein's Cloak and Suit House	200 block East Main
(Leonard M. Klein)	
Women's Ready-to-Wear	202 South Walnut
(Melville L. Altschul)	
Shonfield's Clothing Store	100 West Main
(Louis and Ray Shonfield)	
Max Zeigler & Brothers Junk Yard	620 East Sixth Street
(Max and Harry Zeigler)[18]	

The twenty-two businesses supported an estimated eighty or ninety Jewish families in the town. And while the clothing businesses were most common, others did exist.[19] Both Friedman and Roberts (the owner of the Roberts Hotel) made their money from oil and gas exploration. Burgauer sold type-writers; Pazol, jewelry; and Schwartz, paper. Indorf had a pawn shop. Most of these people had roots in the former Poland or Lithuania and were in occupations far different from those held in Europe by their ancestors.

Even the kinds of clothing stores cannot be predicted from the place of origin or the social class of the owner. Jews from Eastern Europe did not necessarily sell to the business class. Of the three best men's stores in Muncie—Moxie's, Charles Indorf's clothing store, and Marx and Kallmeyer—two were owned by poor Polish-born Jews. Indorf also owned a pawnshop with poorer clients, which was located in a cheaper neighborhood. On the other hand, of the two leading clothing stores for workingmen, one was owned by Sam Gold, a Polish-born Jew, who began his work career in Muncie in a scrap yard in 1907; the other, The Why, belonged to Will Freund, who was born in 1889 in Bromberg, Germany (now Bydgosz, Poland) as the son of a German Jew who emigrated to America in 1894. Both were in a bad neighborhood, one characterized by Freund's son as "the Bowery District—the 'red light' district of Muncie."[20] But poor location did not mean financial failure. Sam Gold became one of the largest Jewish property owners in Muncie from the profits of an establishment described by his daughter as "a workingman's clothing store, and I think it stood him in good stead to be in that type of clothing business."[21]

Business ownership did not guarantee social status; neither did Muncie Jewry lack social division. The deepest divisions were between the socially accepted German-born Jews who arrived first and the "unwashed masses" of Eastern European Jews who came later. The division in Muncie was exacerbated by the fact that the most successful businessmen—Sam Gold and Abe Feinberg—were latecomers from Poland, and less successful Jewish residents were embittered by the newcomers' success. This division seems typical of American Jewry, which, according to William Toll, divided on social rather than ideological grounds.[22] At the same time, however, this division was not quite what the members of the community believed it to be. It was as much a division based on time of arrival and integration into the community as it was on country of origin.

The history of the temple best shows the division which existed in the 1920s between those who had first arrived and those who came later. There had been a Jewish congregation in Muncie since the later nineteenth century. It had always been a Reform congregation (Reform Judaism de-emphasized the ritual practices of Orthodox or traditional Judaism and had been popularized in America by Rabbi Isaac M. Wise. Its center of strength in this country was at the Union of American Hebrew Congregations and Hebrew Union College, both established in Cincinnati in the mid–1870s.) There is no clear written record of just why Muncie had a Reform congregation. Perhaps it was because of the close proximity to Cincinnati, which provided both business and religious connections. In the beginning, as now, Temple Beth El relied upon student rabbis from Hebrew Union College because its size put a full-time rabbi beyond its means. Or perhaps it was a conscious decision that this best suited Jews in Muncie, since the situation in the town made it difficult to follow Jewish dietary laws. Also, most of the Eastern European immigrants were more interested in making a living than in observing Jewish rituals.

When interviewed by Whitney Gordon, the members of the Jewish community in the 1960s believed that the temple was founded by "a very high caliber of German Reform members. And that only later, especially after World War II, did the Orthodox, Eastern European element intrude."[23] Contrary to these beliefs, there had been a considerable number of Orthodox, Eastern European Jews in Muncie at the time of the founding. Further, none of the very old people who were interviewed by Vander Hill and Hoover had come from the Reform tradition; there were even four whose fathers had been Orthodox rabbis or who had studied for the rabbinate in Poland. Even the survey which Gordon made to determine the religious roots of the community belied the comments of those he interviewed. He found that 67 percent of the population had grown up in Orthodox homes, 18 percent in Reform ones, 11 percent in Conservative ones, and 1 percent in Sephardic, Christian, or non-religious homes.[24] Yet the Jewish population of Muncie was a declining one in the 1960s, according to the same persons; there had not been a significant population transfer, which would account for the large proportion of persons who had come from Orthodox homes. The suggestion that German Reform members were solely responsible for founding the temple thus appears untrue, since the Orthodox Eastern European element had such deep roots in the community.

What appears to have happened was that Jews who came to the town, whatever their origin or religious background, joined the congregation if they stayed long enough. Membership in the temple was a sign of integration into the community, both the Jewish and the larger one. This process is illustrated by the fact that when the congregation finally undertook to construct its own building in 1922, the president of the congregation was the Polish-born Charles Indorf, the only Jew who was prominent in local municipal politics. The majority of the members had roots in Eastern Europe as well.

The process of integration into the community was still operative in the 1920s, according to the testimony of persons interviewed by Vander Hill and Hoover. The Samuel Gold family came to Muncie from Indianapolis in 1913; both Samuel and Sadie Gold had come from Eastern Europe. The David Dobrowitz family, which arrived about a decade later, followed the same pattern. Neither family joined the temple in Muncie initially. Instead, both retained their connections with Orthodox congregations in Indianapolis, returning there to worship during the High Holidays. Edith Garfield, a daughter of the Golds, attributed her parents' early refusal to become members of the temple to the fact that "they felt they didn't really fit in with the Jewish community that was there [Muncie] then."[25] The Dobrows (Dobrowitzes) may have been motivated primarily by religious considerations. One informant recalled that the Dobrows tried unsuccessfully to convert the congregation to Orthodox late in the 1920s.[26] Despite the early resistance on the part of the Golds and Dobrows, later both families joined the temple. They had become more a part of the community and no longer looked elsewhere for support. As a son-in-law of the Golds put it, they had mellowed.[27]

The evidence suggests that religious practice was not central to the life of the Jewish community in Muncie. Few Jews refrained from working on Saturday or kept kosher homes. Burle Plank claimed his father never worked a Saturday in his life, nor did his mother violate dietary laws, but the Planks were in the scrap metal and auto parts business, which was somewhat removed from the center of town and was less dependent upon Saturday business.[28] A Jew selling clothes on Walnut Street had more pressure to stay open on the main shopping day of the week. Similarly, keeping kosher was difficult. Those who did—the Planks, Golds, and Dobrows—had to obtain the properly killed meats from Indianapolis or Fort Wayne by interurban or car, since there was no kosher butcher shop in Muncie. For most other families, the effort was not worthwhile.

Most Muncie Jews fit into the pattern of life and work in the town, although Robert Lynd noted one exception when he returned to Muncie in 1935. In reading the newspapers, he found that local Jewish businessmen had taken out an advertisement indicating that their stores would be closed on "religious holidays," an advertisement which he believed would not have been made a decade earlier.[29] This advertising might constitute evidence of a slowing of assimilation and a recognition of ethnic and religious differences in the town.

In the 1920s anti-Semitic and exclusionary sentiments grew in Muncie, as they did in Indiana and the country as a whole. Jews in the nineteenth century participated much more widely in community life than they did in the twentieth century.

One of the most visible symbols of increased prejudice was the arrival of the Ku Klux Klan in Muncie in late 1921. While Jews were a distant third to Catholics and blacks on the Klan's hate list, the presence of the Klan was troubling.[30] According to local tradition, Republican businessmen brought the Klan to Muncie to rid the town of the influence of the corrupt mayor, Rollin "Doc" Bunch, who had been convicted of mail fraud. The first Klavern reputedly met in the office of the local Chamber of Commerce, and the initial membership was largely middle class. The Klan organizers soon broadened the base of membership to include members from the working class, and, by 1923, the Klan claimed a membership of 3,500, which would mean that 10 percent of the population had joined. The Klan exerted more influence than even these substantial numbers might suggest, because members of the secret society held important positions in local government and law enforcement. The chairman of the Board of Public Safety, Philip W. McAbee, was a Klansman, as was the chief of police, Van Benbow. Other members included Delaware Circuit Court Judge Clarence W. Dearth, who was immortalized in *Middletown* for his characterization of automobiles as houses of prostitution on wheels; Frank E. Barclay, a member of the Muncie City Council; Clarence Benadum, a prominent criminal lawyer, former Delaware County prosecuting attorney, amateur novelist, and treasurer of the Klavern; and, most prominent, John Hampton, a local businessman who had become chairman of the Republican Central Committee in 1921, when the Klan first appeared in Muncie, and who became mayor in 1925.[31]

While membership in the Klan was supposedly secret and the power exercised by the informal network of Klansmen concealed, the Klan's presence was highly visible because of its staged public spectacles. The most spectacular of all of these was a parade of some 2,000 members in June 1923. This display of strength, however, backfired when Klan members attempted to coerce bystanders into showing respect for the United States flag draped over the hindquarters of a white horse ridden by a Kamelia. Among those present who felt physically threatened were two prominent Munsonians, a former Congressman, George W. Cromer, and the then–Delaware County prosecuting attorney, J. Frank Mann. The resulting altercation caused the Klan to lose its more respectable members and, along with a schism in the ranks, marked the beginning of the Klan's decline in the city.[32]

During its short career in Muncie, the Klan did shock the Jewish community with its overt anti-Semitism, although the threat was not taken as seriously as might be supposed. However, Jewish residents of the time had no trouble recalling Klan actions.

Perhaps one reason for the lack of fear was that familiar and popular persons belonged. One such individual was the much beloved Muncie Central basketball coach, Pete Jolley, whom Martin Schwartz described as "a great guy but who didn't know much about history or teaching," his major academic responsibility. Jolley confessed to his students that he had joined the Klan but had become convinced that the organization existed only to earn money for its organizers. An even more extreme case was that of the Schwartz housekeeper, who not only joined the Klan but expected her employers to share her pride of membership.[33] If these two individuals had little sense of the Klan's stated message, then the organization had failed to bend its members to its purposes.

Because of the gap between professed aims and actual practice, some members of Muncie's Jewish community were not only friends of Klansmen but, in fact, used that friendship to advantage. One example is the experience of Harry Pazol, who was both a Jew and a newcomer. Pazol bought a jewelry store in Muncie in 1920 after failing to purchase one in his hometown of Cleveland. Friendly and outgoing, Pazol soon made friends in the town and enjoyed the reputation of being a practical joker. One night the joke was on him. He had driven downtown to meet a salesman in his store but had taken his second car, which had expired license plates. After his meeting he discovered his car was missing from its parking place. Fearing it was stolen, he walked to the police station, two short blocks away, to report the theft. When he arrived, he learned that the police had impounded the car and were taunting him about the fact. Pazol called a friend of his who held a high rank in the Klan, and in short order the sergeant returned Pazol's car and let him go without any fine or charge.[34]

Nor was Pazol the only Jewish person who associated with Klansmen. When Archie Lapin moved to Muncie from Hartford City, Indiana, to enter into a law practice, he joined the firm headed by Clarence Benadum, a notorious Klansman. Lapin, however, had only the kindest memories of Benadum.[35]

Still, the Jewish community reacted to the presence of the Klan in a variety of other ways. Rachel Lipp, whose family did not raise her as Jewish, was sent away to a Catholic boarding school in Terre Haute.[36] Sherman Zeigler, whose father owned a scrap yard, recalled that Jews joined Catholics to combat the Klan's economic boycott of both groups: Catholic automobile wreckers agreed to sell scrap only to Jewish yards. This mutual alliance actually improved business.[37] As a boy, Sherman benefited from concerted action by Jewish businessmen to combat anti-Semitism that was apparently not Klan-related. Sherman applied for a paper route when he was twelve years old and was refused because he was Jewish. Although the Zeiglers, by Sherman's own admission, were not really accepted in the Jewish community because of their self-imposed isolation, Sherman's father succeeded in persuading Jewish businessmen who advertised in the paper to inform the Catholic publisher that they would discontinue their ads if such discrimination were not ended. The publisher came to the Zeiglers' home, apologized, and offered Sherman the job.[38]

These tactics, however, did not diminish the prevailing Christian ethos of Muncie, which permeated almost every institution down to the public schools. In the decades between the world wars, the Young Men's Christian Association (YMCA), led by the charismatic boys' work director Herbert A. Pettijohn, sponsored Bible study in the schools and won several national awards for the large number of students enrolled. Part of the attraction for boys was the chance to win a week's stay at Camp Crosley, a summer camp built by the YMCA in the 1920s with funds donated by the Ball family.

The camp attracted Jewish boys who succeeded in winning scholarships. Surprisingly enough, there was little parental objection either to participation in the course or to the week at camp. Part of the reason for lack of concern over participation in Christian exercises was the perception that the values taught were close to those held in Jewish homes, or so Martin D. Schwartz thought: "I would say that our home values were basically middle-class American. . . . There was an enormous emphasis in my family on personal integrity—that you didn't lie, that you were morally straight, the kind of things that H. A. Pettijohn used to teach us at the YMCA."[39]

The sense of shared values between the Jewish and Christian communities was heightened by the lack of interest in traditional religious practice among Muncie's Jewish families. Schwartz's family was not untypical in this regard. His mother, Anna Winick Schwartz, was born in Boston, the daughter of a rabbi who had migrated from Lithuania to Boston before moving to South Africa. She did not share his religious conviction and described herself as never being very religious. Because she was orphaned at an early age and forced to go to work, she may have been so preoccupied with the struggle to survive that religion seemed unimportant.[40] Leo Schwartz also was not concerned about religious matters. He discouraged Martin from learning Hebrew and, according to his son, practiced Judaism perfunctorily.[41]

The case of Harry Pazol paralleled that of Anna Winick. His father, like hers, was a rabbi who migrated from Lithuania to the United States and who lived in strict accordance with Talmudic rules. His life was so exemplary that his son could not imagine anyone being more religious. To Harry, though, this goodness appeared to go unrewarded. In his old age Harry's father journeyed back to the Old World with the intention of visiting his birthplace, as well as Palestine; he died aboard ship before he even got to Lithuania. Based on his father's experience, Harry concluded that religion was of little use and that he should invest little in it.[42]

A third, similar, example is that of the Zeigler family. Sherman Zeigler's father, who was also born in Lithuania, aspired to the rabbinate before he migrated to the United States to escape service in the Tsar's army. By that time he had reacted strongly against religious life, actively discouraging his children from participation as well.[43]

The later arrivals from Eastern Europe were not the only Jews for whom religion had a low priority. Those from Western Europe were equally secular. Rachel Lipp characterized her family in this fashion: "Well, we were not Orthodox Jews. The background was completely German on my father's side, and my mother's was a French background. No, I hate to say it, but very honestly, no, Jewish values were not important in my home."[44] Ann Kallmeyer Secttor had a less strong reaction, but her evaluation was not unlike Rachel Lipp's: "The [Jewish] values were there; my parents observed them; and I think my father had a deeper sense of the meaning [of Jewishness], more so than my mother at the time. But it was never predominant. I never felt any different than anyone else."[45]

To be a Jew in Muncie in the age of the Lynds was to live in a community of flux, one characterized by physical mobility, where status and religious affiliation often depended less on country of origin than on time of arrival, where opportunities to participate fully in community life had shrunk, and where anti-Semitism was openly articulated by the Ku Klux Klan. It meant residing in a community permeated by Christian values, although these values did not appear completely alien. Despite the discrimination and the pressures, Jewish Munsonians regarded themselves as little different from their non-Jewish neighbors. Perhaps, in the end, the Lynds were partially justified in excluding the Jewish community from *Middletown.* Clearly, the values of that community, which were oriented around business success, paralleled those of the larger one.

NOTES

1. Charles E. Harvey, "Robert S. Lynd, John D. Rockefeller, Jr., and *Middletown*," *Indiana Magazine of History*, LXXIX (December 1983), 330–54. See also the second volume (Fall-Winter 1979–80) of the *Journal of the History of Sociology*, which was devoted to Robert S. Lynd.

2. Robert S. and Helen Merrell Lynd, *Middletown: A Study in Contemporary American Culture* (New York, 1929), 8.

3. See Dwight W. Hoover, "From Simpson's Chapel to Grace Baptist Church," in Theodore Caplow, Howard Bahr, Bruce Chadwick et al., *All Faithful People* (Minneapolis, 1983).

4. Nineteen persons were interviewed. The tapes of the interviews and the transcriptions are now in the Center for Middletown Studies at Ball State University. The excerpts which appear in this chapter are verbatim copies from the transcriptions, except where additional material has been added to convey the meaning better. This material is enclosed in brackets.

5. Stephan Thernstrom, "Reflections on the New Urban History," *Daedalus*, C (Spring 1971), 366.

6. Alexander L. Shonfield, *Preface to the History of the Jewish People and a Sketch of Muncie, Indiana* (Fort Wayne, Ind., 1977), 28–29. Shonfield based his statement on an advertisement in *The Muncietonian* that year.

7. Alexander E. Bracken, "Muncie as a Pioneer Community" (Ph.D. dissertation, Department of History, Ball State University, Muncie, Indiana, 1978), 17.

8. General William Harrison Kemper, ed., *A Twentieth Century History of Delaware County, Indiana* (2 vols., Chicago, 1908), I, 146–47, 152, 511; Frank D. Haimbaugh, ed., *History of Delaware County, Indiana* (2 vols., Indianapolis, 1924), I, 308, 365, 462; Thomas B. Helm, *History of Delaware County, Indiana* (Chicago, 1881), 137, 184, 186–87, 196, 221–22, 300.

9. Shonfield, *Preface*, 31.

10. There are contradictions about both Silverburg's first name and his place of birth. In *Emerson's Muncie Directory, 1894–95* (Indianapolis, Ind., 1895), his first name is spelled Hyman. Shonfield says he was born in Prussia, but in *Manufacturing and Mercantile Resources and Industries of the Principal Places of Indiana, Wayne, Henry, Delaware, and Randolph Counties* (n.p., 1881), his birthplace is given as Poland. Of course, at the time these books were published Poland did not exist as a political entity.

11. Shonfield, *Preface*, 22–31; *Emerson's Muncie Directory, 1891–1892*.

12. Judith Morris, "A Focal Study of the Bernard Freund Family" (Seminar paper, Ball State University, Muncie, Indiana, November 1980); Bernard Freund interview, Muncie, Indiana, April 14, 1979; and Pearl Cohen Freund interview, Beverly Hills, California, June 3, 1978.

13. *Emerson's Muncie Directory, 1893–94;* ibid., *1897–98;* ibid., *1899–1900;* Martin D. Schwartz interview, Muncie, Indiana, April 4, 1979; and Anna Schwartz interview, Muncie, Indiana, April 4, 1979.

14. Shonfield, *Preface,* 36; *Emerson's Muncie Directory, 1897–98;* ibid., *1899–1900;* ibid., *1905–06;* ibid., *1921–22.*

15. William Toll, "The 'New Social History' and recent Jewish Historical Writing," *American Jewish History,* LXIX (March 1980), 334.

16. Marc Lee Raphael, *Jews and Judaism in a Midwestern Community: Columbus, Ohio, 1840–1875* (Columbus, Ohio, 1979); William Toll, "The Chosen People in the World of Choice," *Reviews in American History,* VIII (June 1980), 173; see also Judith B. Endelman, *The Jewish Community of Indianapolis, 1849 to the Present* (Bloomington, Ind., 1984).

17. Toll, "The 'New Social History,'" 330.

18. Morris, "Focal Study." This list is not to be taken as completely accurate at any particular date because it represents ownership over at least a ten-year period when stores would often change hands several times.

19. The estimate is Robert Burgauer's, given in his interview, April 25, 1979. This estimate may overstate the number. Far fewer Jews are listed as temple members in Shonfield's history. But, as we have seen, not all Jews were members. Further, the number of members included persons who lived and worked in small towns outside of Muncie.

20. Bernard Freund interview.

21. Edith Garfield interview, Indianapolis, Indiana, May 14, 1979.

22. Toll, "The 'New Social History,'" 336.

23. Whitney Gordon, *Community in Stress* (New York, 1964), 8.

24. Ibid., 105.

25. Garfield interview.

26. Shonfield interview.

27. Archie Lapin interview, Muncie, Indiana, February 27, 1979.

28. Burle Plank interview, Muncie, Indiana, February 22, 1979.

29. Robert S. and Helen Merrell Lynd, *Middletown in Transition: A Study in Cultural Conflicts* (New York, 1937), 462.

30. The best general treatment of the Klan after World War I is Kenneth T. Jackson's *The Ku Klux Klan in the City, 1915–1930* (New York, 1967). For the Klan in Indiana, see James H. Madison, *Indiana Through Tradition and Change: A History of the Hoosier State and Its People, 1920–1945* (Indianapolis, Ind., 1982), 44–75.

31. Carrolyle M. Frank, "Politics in Middletown: A Reconsideration of Municipal Government and Community Power in Muncie, Indiana, 1925–1935" (Ph.D. dissertation, Department of History, Ball State University, Muncie, Indiana, 1974), 58–84.

32. Ibid., 58–59.

33. Ibid.

34. Mort Pazol interview.

35. Lapin interview.
36. Rachel Lipp interview, Fort Wayne, Indiana, March 2, 1979.
37. Sherman Zeigler interview, Muncie, Indiana, February 26, 1979.
38. Ibid.
39. Martin D. Schwartz interview.
40. Anna Schwartz interview.
41. Martin D. Schwartz interview.
42. Harry Pazol interview, Louisville, Kentucky, May 31, 1979.
43. Zeigler interview.
44. Lipp interview.
45. Ann Kallmeyer Secttor interview, Marion, Indiana, April 2, 1979.

❊ Middletown Jews ❊

❊ 1 ❊

The Beautiful Steak with the Pat of Butter

MORT PAZOL

Mort Pazol, with his brother, Herb, was proprietor of Pazol's Jewelry, the last of the old Jewish-family-operated stores that once dominated Walnut Street. His father, Harry Pazol (1887–1982), was a cousin of the legendary Hollywood producer David O. Selznick, and moved to Los Angeles after World War II. Mort Pazol was instrumental in racial integration of job sites in Muncie after World War II.

My grandfather settled in Cleveland very early—probably in the late 1870s. He went back and forth to Lithuania several times. In fact, my father was conceived during one of the trips back there. But dad didn't get to this country until about 1895.

My dad worked in jewelry stores in Cleveland from around 1920. He was a good salesman and he saved some money. One of his friends was an auctioneer who would buy up stores and get rid of them one way or another. Dad told him if he ever found a good store to let him know. He ran an auction here in Muncie and told Dad he had a good store for him. Dad believed him and we came here in 1920.

In Cleveland maybe half our neighbors were Jewish, but here there were none. Maybe I was too young and innocent to know what culture shock was. There was no kosher butcher shop around. That was a shock to my mother. Although she didn't keep kosher, she'd insist on kosher meat. There was a *shochet*[1] here in the late 1920s or early '30s, but it didn't last long.

My mother helped out in the store quite a bit, so we had somebody to take care of us and cook. I remember my mother came home one time and she saw the beautiful big steak with the pat of butter soaking into it. It turned her stomach, and she threw it out. Eventually our cook learned not to do that.

My mother and father both got as far away from the old Jewish traditions as fast as they could. My father's father was a *rav*,[2] and they had to do everything exactly right. Dad got tired of that as a very young child. Mother was the oldest of six girls, and she couldn't see any sense in keeping all the dishes separate. She too got away from it as fast as she could.

I went through the religious school at Beth El Temple up to age thirteen—the age of confirmation. We didn't have *bar mitzvah* in those days in Reform congregations.

*

I remember the Ku Klux Klan very well. We lived at one of the entrances to town, and one time when the Klan was holding a big conclave in Muncie, they had their people in full regalia at the entrances to town to show the brothers where to go. I remember seeing this one man not fifty feet from me practically all day long. But the Klan itself, at least in Muncie, was not nearly as anti-Jewish as it was anti-Catholic and anti-black. There were so few of us that we didn't bother them.

I remember one winter night my father drove downtown with a salesman to go over the salesman's line. He parked in

---

[1] A ritual slaughterer of kosher meat.
[2] A Hasidic holy man.

front of the store and worked with the salesman for a couple of hours. The car wasn't his regular car, and the license plate had expired. When he left the store, the car was missing. When he went to the police station to report his car stolen, the desk sergeant laughed at him: "We really got you," he said. "You didn't have the right license plate on it, and it's going to cost you, and you can't have it tonight."

Well, Dad got on the phone and called a friend of his who he knew was high in the Klan. The Klansman said, "Let me talk to that sergeant." And he did. I guess the sergeant really got told off, because he gave Dad his car without any charge or fine of any type. And I think this was pretty much typical. Those big boys were in the Klan for the money and the political power, not for the ideology.

The anti-Semitism I have felt has been more of a social thing—I wasn't invited to parties that I would expect to be invited to. That's really about it. And that's definitely changed quite a bit in the last ten or fifteen years. Now I have no feeling of being discriminated against at all.

*

When it came to housing, Westwood was always closed to our people, and Kenmore was at one time. Those were the two best residential neighborhoods. I also know there have been a few others. But I don't think there's anything like that today.

I remember in 1932 or '33, a friend of my father's had a very lovely home in Westwood, and the guy was broke. He told Dad how much he wanted for it, and Dad said, "Fine." Now, in those days you couldn't take your money out of the building-and-loan companies in quantity—I think they held you to $50 a month, or something like that. Dad had enough money to pay for this house in the building-and-loan company that held the mortgage on it. He and his friend went down there, and there was no way he could get his money out or transfer the mortgage or anything like that. And you know, within the next week that house was sold to someone else.

*

When we came here, if you wanted to see 75 to 85 percent of the male members of the Jewish community, all you had to do was walk down Walnut Street and drop into the stores. Man, how that's changed! Now there's one Jewish merchant in Muncie.

The social life was very active then. We came here before the temple was built, but there was a male organization called the Eureka Club, which had its headquarters on the corner of Mulberry and Main streets. The men used to play poker there, except when there were religious services or a community affair of some type. The women played quite a bit of bridge and, shortly thereafter, mah jongg. Of course, the women's games took place in homes. Usually there'd be four couples: The four men would play one game and the four women another. Rarely would both sexes play games together.

We had the Indiana Union of Jewish Youth from the time I arrived until the late '30s; I was president in the '30s. The whole Jewish community of Anderson, Marion, and Muncie were very close together then, visited back and forth and knew each other quite well from top to bottom. That contact probably faded because we [Jews] became more socially accepted in our individual communities—in country clubs, things like that.

In the early '20s there were a few Jewish members of the Delaware Country Club. But when they found their friends couldn't join, they dropped out. The service clubs—Rotary, Lions, Kiwanis, and so on—did not have Jewish membership.

*

Right after World War II, the American Jewish Committee set up a program in some 46 cities, including Muncie, to teach the leading of discussions. The important thing in leading a discussion, of course, is to make sure that the discussion doesn't stray completely off the subject. But probably even more important is to see that everybody present contributes in some way. Because I had participated in this program, in 1947 or '48,

when I was chairman of the executive committee of the local
NAACP chapter, our executive committee meetings were extremely well attended—from twenty to thirty people at every
meeting, and everybody participating in the discussion.

Very early in the war, the Workers' Service Division of the
Works Progress Administration came to the CIO Council and
the A.F. of L. Central Labor Union and a black group whose
name I don't remember, and asked that these three groups form
an organization to help integrate blacks into the work force.
Our major success was having a young black hired in a skilled
capacity as an electrician at Durham Manufacturing Company,
which made shells at that stage and had been strictly segre-
gated.

Also, as an organization, we asked our affiliated organizations—in my case, the CIO Council—to pass resolutions to negotiate the hiring of blacks (we called them "colored people"
at that stage). I can't say that that worked out particularly well
with their respective employers. For instance, at Warner Gear,
when the delegation went in to negotiate, the employer gave
them a choice: either blacks or women. They took women.
Warner Gear had always had a few black sweepers, but I think
it was well after the war before they hired any blacks on the
assembly line or in a skilled trade.

*

A real estate man I knew came to me and said, "Mort, there's
this property out here, an old Ball family farm—a beautiful
piece of property. I think it would make a beautiful country
club, and the people in the Jewish community would be interested in building one out here."

The idea didn't sound too bad to me, and I asked around
and we got a group together, discussed it and decided to do it.
The original money was put up by members of the Jewish community, and we went on from there.

Of course, it [the Green Hills Country Club] was never a
Jewish country club. There was no thought of having exclusively Jewish membership. But the original financing came

from the Jewish community. One thing I personally was unhappy about, and I know several other people were, too: We
were never strong enough to break down [racial] segregation,
so we never had black membership.

*

Believe it or not, I'm rather proud of our Jewish community. I've read statements from sociologists and other experts
who know what goes on in communities like ours, which fade
away and cease to exist. Well, Muncie's community hasn't, and
it won't. There's been a tremendous change in the makeup of
our community. Up until fairly recently, we were small merchants, with an occasional store manager coming and going.
Today that's all gone. We have a few professional men, which
we didn't have before. Ball State University has attracted quite
a number of Jewish faculty members, some of whom are active community members. So I feel quite optimistic about the
future of Muncie's Jewish community, within its limitations. I
don't think it will ever flower to the extent of being interna-
tionally known. But it will exist and offer what it has to those
who come around it.

It's just not practical for us to have a full-time rabbi here.
We've tried that. But the only men we were able to get were
young men who, on occasion, left us in the middle of the year
if they had a decent offer, or men who were failures in other
places before they got here. As small as we are, we can't con-
ceivably offer enough money.

With the students from Hebrew Union College in Cincinnati, we have people who, we think, have some capability, and
who will stay at least as long as their contract holds.

There is a section of Beech Grove Cemetery that has been
allotted to the Jewish community—as far as I know, for as long
as there was a Beech Grove Cemetery.

Today there's a Muncie-Anderson Hadassah chapter, and
a B'nai B'rith men's group. I've been an officer of B'nai B'rith
most of the time from about 1937 until now—president several times, secretary several times, usually chairman of the

nominating committee. I used to go to state conventions and the district convention. As a matter of fact, fifteen years ago I bumped into a guy from South Bend who said when he thinks of Muncie, he thinks of Mort Pazol. But B'nai B'rith here is about as inactive as you can get. We pay our dues, we hold a meeting most months, and we do nothing.

Both of my children are gone. Our community's children have to a very large degree intermarried. Look, the more things you have in common with your children and your family and their mate's family, the nicer it is. I wouldn't go any farther than that. As far as I'm concerned, religion is just one of many factors, and not the most important.

FEBRUARY 21, 1979

❧ 2 ❧

"I'm the Jew You're Talking About"

BEN HERTZ

Ben Hertz was chief executive of Midwest Towel Inc., a linen-supply business which he started in Muncie with his father, Morris Hertz, in 1937, when he was nineteen. By 1979, when this interview was conducted, it had grown from two truck routes to a fleet of about 125 cars and trucks delivering rental linens throughout Indiana and parts of Ohio and Michigan. One of his two sons joined him in the business.

My father was born in a small town in Poland,[1] but his father died at the age of forty, and his widow came over and settled in New York. My Dad had a brother in the linen-supply business in Detroit, and the two of them moved to Flint, Michigan, and started a linen supply business with a partner—

---

[1] Most references to Poland in these interviews refer to historical and/or present-day Poland. Poland was largely partitioned among Russia, Germany, and Austria between 1772 and 1795 and did not exist at all as a political entity between 1863 and 1918.

a rental service on linens and aprons, towels, table linens, sheets, pillow cases—anything in the cotton-goods line.

My father knew a man named Shorty Grimes who had been working for linen supply companies all over the Middle West and decided to go on his own in Muncie—a very small business, a one- or two-truck outfit. He didn't even have his own processing facilities. In 1937 my father heard that Grimes owed so much money that his suppliers were going to close him up. My dad sent me down to this area to look it over—I was nineteen at the time—and it seemed to me that we could open up business in a lot of outlying towns that Grimes wasn't even serving. So I told my father to just go ahead and give Grimes whatever he wanted for the business. The comical part is that Grimes went all over town telling people that this was the first time in history that an Irishman had screwed a Jew.

When we first came here, I would say that the non-Jewish community really didn't know what a Jew looked like, even though they did business with them every day, such as in Pazol's Jewelry Store or Stanley Schuster's clothing store.

[*Pauline Hertz*: The nurses came to take a look at me when I gave birth to Jack, because they had never seen a Jew.]

We had competitive problems when we first came to town, strictly from a Jewish standpoint. *Strictly from a Jewish standpoint.* We were told point-blank when the customer quit and went to a company out in New Castle that they had never done business with a Jew before and they weren't going to start. They were talking to me and didn't know I was Jewish.

We were small in those days and I did everything, including driving a route, and the first six or seven customers I went to in the morning had quit. They said, "We don't want your service any more," and I couldn't get them to tell me why. But the last one I went to that morning said, "Well, we don't want to do business with a Jew."

I said, "What's the difference in the color of our skin?"

"Nothing. Why?"

"I'm the Jew you're talking about," I said.

"You've got to be kidding," he said.

"Did you ever buy any jewelry?" I said.

"Yes," he replied.

"Who do you buy it from?"

"Harry Pazol."

"Do you follow baseball?" I said.

"Yes, I love baseball."

"Who's the best hitter in the American League today?"

"Hank Greenberg."

"Did you know he was a Jew?"

"Aw, come on," he said. "You've got to be pulling my leg."

This is what went on here. Remember that the Klan was strong here. An attorney here, Clarence Benadum, was one of the Klan's big leaders. They had an office downtown. A newspaper here called *The X-Ray* blasted Jews all over hell's half-acre. This was the education that people got about Jews.

When Jack was an infant and Pauline and I were first looking for a home, in 1942, Pauline called Bob Dailey, one of the leading real estate agents here in town. She told him what areas we wanted to go into, and two of the areas she talked about were called Kenmore and Westwood. And he point-blank told her that we wouldn't be happy there and nobody in that area would play with our kids. It all came out of the blue to us. She didn't know what he was referring to at first.

*

I tried to keep my values so the non-Jewish community couldn't criticize Ben Hertz as far as my business dealings or anything I did in town—especially after I was married. I may have tried to get away with a little shenanigans before I was married, but never any dishonesty. What bothered me about some of the Jewish business people here in town was some of their business ethics.

I don't mean to say that Jews have bad business ethics—they're no different than anybody else's. But it used to bother me when I knew that somebody in our [Jewish] community wasn't completely 100 percent above-board in his business dealings with others—to the point where in the past there have been some people that I just refuse to even associate with or speak to. Because I always felt that whatever somebody else did that was wrong rubbed off on me—only because I was in the minority. And that's true of every minority.

If I do something wrong, for instance, they will say, "Well, what do you expect from a Jew?" or "Those goddamn Jews are all alike." And it's the same thing if somebody does wrong within the black community. It's not "Ben Hertz is a no-good son of a bitch," but "What do you expect from the Jews?"

They don't say that in your WASP community. They will say, "John Jones is no good." But we get treated differently, so therefore we have to act differently. We have to bend over backwards to be good citizens, because other people won't let us be anything else. Do you understand what I'm saying?

I'm very proud of the fact that here in Muncie, I can walk in anywhere and just make a deal on a handshake for thousands and thousands and thousands of dollars—with my purveyors, with the banks, with anything. But because of my self-consciousness of who I am, I recognize what people will say. If I do something wrong, it will rub off on Marty Schwartz, it will rub off on Bernard Freund, it will rub off on Bob Burgauer and this entire Jewish community. Therefore, I do my utmost to stay above-board at all times. The fact of the matter is, it probably cost me thousands of dollars a year to do it.

*

In the 1930s and '40s the social life of Muncie's Jewish community revolved around the temple. Whenever there was a social function it was in the basement of the temple, in the recreation room. Or in somebody's home. My dad was very active with the temple and the United Jewish Appeal, which took care not only of the Zionists but also poor Jews and the old folks' home and that sort of thing. We always had a fund here to help out any indigent Jew who might come through the area.

My family was Orthodox and kept a kosher home. So did the Dobrows, the Barticks, Sam [and Sadie] Gold—quite a few of them. The meat used to come up by bus from Indianapolis, once a week. I would say the butcher in Indianapolis did quite a business here, between selling lox and bagels and Jewish rye breads and that sort of thing.

*

We didn't get the Klan out of town until after the [Second World] war. We had a gentleman here named Don Galinsky— a veteran and war hero, I think. He and a few of us went down to the American Legion, because we didn't want to take on the Klan ourselves as Jews. The American Legion got the owner of the building to cancel the Klan's office lease.

[Delaware] Country Club was closed to Jews until just a few years ago. The Elks Club was closed to Jews, even though the [national] Grand Exalted Ruler at one time was a Jew by the name of Stein. Some members of the Elks came into my office one day and said they were just sick about it, and would I write a letter to this Grand Exalted Ruler and tell him that Jews aren't allowed into this Elks Club?

I refused. "If you fellows feel that way," I said, "why don't *you* write?" But you see, they didn't want to get involved. I guess they were afraid they'd get themselves thrown out of the Elks.

*

I'm not a religious-type Jew. I really don't know what goes on down at the temple. If you would ask my 37-year-old son, he would know more. By the way, he has intermarried. He married a Jewish girl the first time around, and now he's married to a lovely girl, but she adopted the Jewish faith, and I think there's no one who knows more about what goes on in the Jewish community. Right now she's president of the sister-hood and works very hard. I think that some of our daughters who adopted the religion are the worst kind of Jews that there are—they always push you to be Jewish.

The Muncie Club just opened up its membership to Jews here not too long ago. Some people say there has been an in-crease of toleration. On the surface, yes. But what's happening if you scratch the surface? My daughter-in-law said just the other day that there are some remarks being tossed around now in town. She said people give her remarks because as far as they're concerned, she's not Jewish—even though she turned Jewish, they still remember her as a non-Jew.

Remember in 1973, the Saudis shut off our oil supply because of the Israeli war with Syria? Ever since then, we've been paying through the nose for gasoline. A lot of people are blaming it on the State of Israel. And what's the State of Israel? Jews. I'm not a citizen of Israel. I'm an American of the Jewish faith, and that's the way I want to be known. I preach this to a lot of people who say that Judaism is a nationality.

I take issue with the word "toleration." If somebody's just going to tolerate you, then there is still some anti-Semitism. I can't believe that the only time anybody ever found anti-Semitism was when they went to look for it. When it came to find you, believe me, it came to find you in some instances.

*

I think that most of us who can get out [of Muncie], leave. At least for a good portion of the winter. The Burgauers are now beginning to go south. And the Dobrows, and the Hertzes. I'll tell you what this town taught me as far as business is concerned. It taught me how to organize a business so I wouldn't have to be here. I don't dislike Muncie, but I don't want to be here twelve months a year. Frankly, there isn't a hell of a lot of social life here for my wife and me. There aren't too many people that we see in Muncie within the Jewish community any more.

*

From my viewpoint—and remember, I'm not here much, I'm out of town about seven months a year—I think there's a weakening of the Jewish community here. Maybe the Jews feel more secure with non-Jewish people now. It's like cows herding together in a field when they know a storm is approaching: Now there are no storms. I look at a Jewish community in the past which used to live together and socialize together and never went outside of their own people.

We have seen and we will see more intermarriages. It happened to me. It just so happened that my daughter-in-law did convert and has become very active. But I think that a good portion of our Jewish community is made up of that. You know, there are some who don't even acknowledge that they're Jewish, really. But if anybody starts any problem anywhere, they'll be Jews—because they'll find them and make them realize it.

MAY 15, 1979

🞷 3 🞷

The Klansman's Beneficiary

IDA AND ARCHIE LAPIN

*Archie Lapin practiced law in Muncie from 1931. He served
as president of Muncie's Temple Beth El and of the local B'nai
B'rith chapter. His wife, Ida, eldest daughter of Sam and Sadie
Gold, was a lifelong resident of Muncie. An interview with
Ida's sister, Edith Garfield, also appears in this book.*

Ida: My mother came from Russia and my father from Poland, around 1905. From Europe they came to Indianapolis,
and my father worked there a couple of years as a peddler. He
was peddling around and he met Max Zeigler, and they became partners in a junk business for several years. When that
didn't go too well, my father opened a men's furnishings store
in downtown Muncie in 1909. He owned it by himself, and
my mother worked there part of the time. I was born in 1913
and helped out in the store when I was fourteen or fifteen, but
I got married quite early, so that ended my career as a saleslady.

Archie: My father and mother both emigrated from a bor-
der town in Russian Poland in 1902. He was a tailor by trade
and graduated upward from a tailor shop in Chicago to owning a manufacturing concern that made ladies' dresses and

undergarments. In the late 1920s many small towns engaged in a sort of promotion to induce factories from Chicago to come to other areas where labor was cheaper. In the late 1920s my father was contacted by the Chamber of Commerce of Hartford City,[1] which approached him with various financing programs and a place for his business, so he ran his business there until the Depression hit in 1929.

Hartford City had maybe five or six Jewish families, and it was customary to come to Muncie to attend the temple and take part in Jewish community events. So in that way my parents became acquainted with Ida's parents, and through them we became acquainted. My father became a member of B'nai B'rith and would come to Muncie to their meetings, and that's how he became acquainted with Mr. Gold. Then followed the usual course of their coming to Hartford City to visit us, and our coming from Hartford City to visit them, and that's how the romance developed. We were married in 1930.

By that time Ida's dad was well established in Muncie. He was very successful in real estate and that sort of thing. He continued to operate his store there and retired in 1949, after forty years in business. He catered to the working class, and if anything his type of business was not hurt by the Depression; it was helped, because of the cheaper merchandise he sold. There were other Jewish merchants in Muncie who sold better types of merchandise. When you think of men's and women's clothing, and jewelry, retailing in Muncie at that time was largely dominated by Jews.

My father remained in manufacturing, and when the Depression hit he returned to Chicago. He never came back to this part of Indiana, except to visit.

*

Ida: I wouldn't say I went to Sunday school much in Muncie. See, my folks were quite religious—they were Orthodox—and

---

[1]A county seat town of 8,000, twenty miles north of Muncie.

our community was more Reform. We were friendly and all that, but when it came to the High Holidays, we went to Indianapolis, because there was an Orthodox congregation there. The Zeiglers and my aunt and uncle, the Watkinses, went there too. At that time religious life was quite important in our family.

Archie: You should say that your parents mellowed a great deal with time and became quite active in our temple. Her father became a member of B'nai B'rith, and her mother became a member of the sisterhood. So we've had a lot of activity around the temple over the years.

Ida: My parents gradually went from more Orthodox to more Reform. You make acquaintances, after all, and you want to be with your friends. Going to Indianapolis for just two or three days a year for our holidays was a little hard.

Archie: They would still go into Indianapolis, but less frequently as the years went by.

*

Ida: I really didn't have enough education; that's my gripe. I went through [Muncie] Central High School, that's all, because I was married when I was quite young. My husband has his education.

Archie: Yes, I had a high school education, I had two years of pre-law and three years at John Marshall Law School in Chicago. It was a matter of going to school days and working afternoons and evenings until I graduated. Those were the years when the movie houses were developing. The firm of Balaban & Katz was very big, and what better job for a boy who gets out of school about 3:30 or 4 o'clock than to be an usher? I spent several years in several Chicago theaters—one was the Chicago Theater on State Street, and another was the Uptown Theater on Broadway. And I worked in the Post Office for a couple of years. Saturdays I worked as a shoe salesman in downtown stores—O'Connor & Goldberg, the Boston Store, the Fair.

I came back to Indiana to practice because my father was still in Hartford City. I figured that perhaps my training could help him in the business. In the meantime, I met Ida, and business started to go bad. And when my father decided to go back to Chicago, I started to think about actually hanging my shingle out, which I did in Muncie in 1931, and I have been practicing here ever since. I'm not quite the dean of the legal community here, but I'm close.

*

When I came here the Klan was in decline. But it still had a lot of members. I went to work in the office of Mr. [Clarence] Benadum, an attorney who had formerly been a very active Klan organizer. In my experience and contact with Benadum I myself have never felt anything which would give me the impression he was anti-Semitic. The talk was that he went into the Klan for the money.

In any event, he was my benefactor. He gave me a chance to get acquainted. And I didn't know of any Klan activities when I came, but I'd read a lot about it. But a few years later a man came to the community by the name of Court Asher, who evidently had been a friend of Benadum's, and I met him in Benadum's office. He was said to be a newspaperman and a reporter on a Chicago newspaper; then he got in trouble with the law and did time; then he came back to Muncie and started this *X-Ray* right-wing newspaper, attacking people as Communists and blasphemers. Even though I was in Benadum's office and was friendly with him, Asher still did not deny me the publicity and the notoriety of his newspaper. I made the front-page quite often.

To me it was funny, the things that were said. Asher didn't have much of a following; he was looked upon as a crackpot, pure and simple. He had some guys who were anti-Semitic who were feeding him money, and he used it for his paper. But it was vicious and untrue. It came out weekly, and I'm sure that some people might have been influenced by it. We had some small incidents that we thought about referring to our B'nai B'rith Anti-Defamation League, but we decided to ignore him, because to recognize him and fight him was just giving him publicity and ammunition. But I can't say that there was any incident with anyone with whom I had any relationships that would give me a reason to believe they were being anti-Semitic.

*

Ida: I don't think the Jewish community in Muncie has much future, because I don't think there's enough coming in and I don't think the people are as active as we were. They're not that interested. The older people, I think we were a little more dedicated. I don't think the younger generation wants to put themselves out as much as we did. We really worked.

Archie: I disagree that the future is a black one for the Jewish community. I think it's been changing, but it's not necessarily less active. Formerly the community was made up of businessmen and shopkeepers on Walnut Street. Now the people coming into town are coming in as a result of the University [Ball State]. They're more faculty people and perhaps a little more educated. The fact that we think it's not quite as active, I'd say, is the fact that we're not quite as active as we were. Because we don't relate too well to the younger people. But from what I understand, they are active and they do get together.

Ida: They do get together, but have they advanced? When I was a young girl, our congregation had just a small room upstairs, on Main Street. The older generation wanted a temple. They strived for something better, for something bigger. So from the time I was a child to an adult there was quite an advancement. The community worked to the point where we had a temple. What are the newer people, the young people—what are they striving for? I don't see anything better than what we had.

Archie: That's largely because the community has gotten smaller, don't you think?

Ida: That's right, but what have they done to elevate it? I think the older people progressed much more rapidly than the younger group. They've stopped.

Archie: But with fewer people, and fewer people of means,

they have maintained the temple, they have maintained the Sunday school, they do have a rabbi every other week. Over the years, it's true, we have worked to improve the temple, to buy equipment for the kitchen, to maintain a regular rabbi and various other projects. But the fact remains that they're maintaining a Sunday school now with fewer people and less per capita income but greater overall expenses. I think Ida means there isn't any apparent progress, but I think those who are here are maintaining a fair degree of activity.

Ida: We didn't have such a large group when I was a little girl, but they really worked. There isn't that much going on now, Arch. I'm sorry, I disagree with you.

April 17, 1979

4

At Home with Gentiles

RACHEL SHONFIELD LIPP

Rachel Lipp lived most of her adult life in the larger city of Fort Wayne, an hour's drive north of Muncie.

My [Shonfield] grandparents came from Oberkerkan, Germany, in 1852 and settled in Springfield, Ohio. Then they moved to Frankfort, Indiana. The house that my grandmother built in Muncie is still standing at the corner of Cherry and Main. It's about to fall down. I was by there not too long ago and I felt very bad. It was a beautiful, beautiful home. In fact, she built two right behind it on Cherry Street.

My grandfather went into the clothing business when he came to Muncie. I think all his boys went into it too. I have an uncle, Sam, who was even in the business in New Castle [Indiana]. Most of them, this was what they did. Uncle Lew, my father, and Uncle Sam, they all did the same thing.

My father was in the retail business with his brothers. Then he branched out and went into the business of organizing and putting on sales for people in the clothing business. He went from town to town; they wanted something put together, and that was Dad's job. He must have done his office work at home. He died when I was three and a half years old.

*

I had no problems in Muncie whatsoever. My friends were all gentile friends, except, when I was real young, Bessie Roberts, Wayne Roberts, Cullie Roberts, Bill Deutsch. I don't know what's happened to them. It was a very small Jewish community—not many young people. But I went with all these gentile people.

I even went to the Christian Science Sunday school. I went to the Methodist Sunday school. Because we didn't have a rabbi all the time, and I had quite a bit of Christian Scientist friends, and our family allowed me to do this. It didn't bother them.

Oh, I was confirmed at the temple. But you see, we had a rabbi only on the weekend, so often there was no rabbi for the confirmation class. I don't believe the temple sponsored any youth activities. They were a small community, and they weren't doing the things then that they do today.

I was too young to realize much about the Klan, but I know that that's why I was taken out of Muncie [in the 1920s] and put in school at St. Mary of the Woods, outside of Terre Haute. After I was older I was told that was the reason. My Uncle John Cherry in Danville[1] sent me there. After four years at St. Mary's I went to a junior college in Gulfport, Mississippi, and then back to Danville. My uncle was in the ice cream manufacturing business there, and after I finished school I worked down in the office. I didn't return to Muncie until 1939, for about two and a half years.

We were not Orthodox Jews. The background was completely German on my father's side, and my mother's was a French background. It was a very tolerant family, with a lot of intermarriage. The uncle and aunt that I lived with [in Danville]—she was my father's sister—she married a gentile. And they did everything in this world for me. My other aunt, Carrie, was married to a gentile. My brother has been married

---

[1] A county seat town about twenty miles west of Indianapolis.

to a gentile girl. I grew up without any feeling of strangeness among gentile people. I expect I feel more at home with them [as a result]. My friends in Danville were always gentiles. They're still my friends; I'm still in touch with them.

I knew that anti-Semitism existed, very definitely. But I was never made to feel uncomfortable, ever—never in Muncie, and never in Danville or Fort Wayne.

*

The aunt with whom I lived in Danville became ill with cancer, and the family had for years come up here [Fort Wayne] to Dr. Rosenthal. He was a very fine doctor, and Julia was at St. Joe's Hospital here under his care. She didn't want to go any place else. I don't know how long she was in the hospital, but I was ill in Danville—I had acute arthritis and a strep infection—so I came up and stayed here too, and Dr. Rosenthal took care of me. Then I met Phil, my husband, here and was married here.

Fort Wayne is a much larger Jewish community [than Muncie's], and for that reason there is a great deal more done in Jewish education than there ever was in Muncie. Jewish children today are really being educated in religion. They're stressing it. And I think it's important. But I think they have to be taught tolerance on our part as well as we expect tolerance from the gentiles. I do think there's more tolerance in America today [among religious groups]. I think the war [World War II] did it. The whole world learned a lesson.

*

Of my three children, Stanley took over his father's business. It's under a different name now: Carpetland. Stan was the first of the franchisees—he and Rick Meyer, who is of German descent too. My husband has been in the business for eighteen years.

My middle child, Julie, went to the University of Missouri, came out and took her little portfolio and walked into Chicago, got herself a job and has been there ever since. She went with Montgomery Ward first and then to the *Chicago Tribune,*

selling the newspapers to the public school system and going
into the classrooms. Then Julie went to the *Chicago Daily News*,
selling advertising. When the *News* closed, she went right over
to the *Sun-Times*.

David, my youngest, is a scholar, he really is. He's teaching black history at Martin Luther King High School in Chicago. But he may be leaving. He's a little scared at what's going on in the school. They don't want whites to teach black
history. But the principal wants David, he loves his work, he
gets along beautifully with his students. He says, "As long as
I teach, it's going to be at Martin Luther King High School."

MARCH 7, 1979

❊ 5 ❊

"Muncie Will Always Be Home to Me"

BUD ROTH

Dr. Morton (Bud) Roth, a practicing optometrist in Muncie since 1948, married a non-Jew and largely dropped out of involvement with the Jewish community.

My maternal grandfather, Sam Schwartz, was born in Lithuania and emigrated to the U.S., where he married my grandmother, Fannie Epstein. My Grandfather Schwartz started as a peddler of shoestrings and shoelaces and sundry items until he garnered enough funds to open a shoe store and came to Muncie during the gas boom just before the turn of the century.

My father's parents, Silas and Yetta Roth, were from Austria-Hungary and lived in Newport, Kentucky, across the Ohio River from Cincinnati. My Grandfather Roth was in the clothing manufacturing business. I'm not too clear as to how my father found his way to Muncie, except that, as I recall his telling me, he had been traveling on the road and he called on my Grandfather Schwartz in some manner, and in turn met my mother, Bessie Schwartz.

In my early recollections, my parents always seemed to be struggling financially. My father worked for my Grandfather Schwartz as a shoe clerk and was more or less manager of his shoe store here. The remuneration was none too good. My mother essentially never worked, except in her home. She and her mother were fastidious housekeepers, to the point that it made living at home burdensome, because if anything was out of place it was really a problem. She and my grandmother both gained a reputation in the Jewish community as probably having the cleanest houses around.

My father was extremely well liked in this community—a very generous man, a warm person, much more so than my mother was. Mother—again, being preoccupied with the family and keeping the house cleaned up properly—was not active in the community. My father, being always in the retail business, enjoyed people, enjoyed working with them. But I think he was frustrated because he had never been a financial success. He was a poor financial planner. He didn't lack intelligence, and he certainly worked hard and put in long hours. But he never seemed to get ahead. Many of the Jews he knew seemed to have succeeded economically, and I think that was one of the reasons he was so terribly frustrated.

He had a younger brother, George Roth, who came here and started in the women's ready-to-wear business and became quite successful. During the Depression, George came to my father's rescue many times. I can recall many times when we didn't have enough food on the shelf or enough coal to keep the house warm, and my Uncle George would always send the necessary funds. I'm sure there were always certain strings attached to this help, and it was very belittling to my father and bothersome to my mother that he had to accept this kind of charity. George and my father had another younger brother, Morton Roth—same name as mine—who lived in Anderson and was very successful in ready-to-wear.

My parents, as far as we kids were concerned, didn't have a very warm relationship. We never saw one of them strike the other, but there were a lot of arguments, a lot of name-call-ing—that sort of thing. A lot of the conflict may have had to do with the financial problems, and with seeing a high percent-age of their very good friends doing much better than they did—it was a bitter struggle for them. My mother, having come from a background of better means, wasn't accustomed to this and couldn't acclimate herself.

My Grandfather Schwartz, who was a reasonably success-ful merchant, lost most everything during the Depression and never really recovered his financial posture. Eventually, in fact—when I was in junior high and high school—my dad left my grandfather's shoe store and went to work for my Uncle George.

Later on, when I was in college, Dad was in the jewelry business. He had been asked to work for a cousin of his, Lawson Jaffe, who had set up a jewelry business here in partnership with Morton Standt, a cousin of mine on my father's side. Dad worked for Lawson Jaffe for many, many years—another situ-ation where he put in many long hours and his work was not rewarded financially. It was pretty bad.

After I had gone into the service, I believe, Dad left Lawson Jaffe because my Uncle George had asked him to come into business with him. George was at a stage where he wanted to retire to Florida, even though he was younger than my dad. So George moved to Florida and my dad managed George's business for him, and then George died. Supposedly, George had made arrangements—it was all oral—that my father would be left the store, or a good financial interest in the store. But as it turned out, George's wife, my Aunt Bennette, had different ideas, and my dad ended up with almost nothing. I think she finally made a financial settlement which was very paltry.

At that time my dad was in his late fifties or early sixties—not in very good health. He was smoking himself to death. He went to work for an automobile company, selling cars for a while, and then he reached sixty-five and was able to get his Social Security. He and mother sold the house here and moved to a small home in Hollywood, Florida. But not too long after they moved down there, he was diagnosed with lung cancer, and he died about eighteen months later.

Because a younger sister of mine had moved to Florida, we decided it would be better if my mother stayed there. But she missed Muncie terribly—it was a delayed state of depression—and about a year after Dad died she became so mentally unbalanced that we brought her back to Muncie and put her under psychiatric treatment until she regained her composure again. Once she was back on an even keel, we packed her up and shipped her back down to Florida, and she had her own little apartment down there until she suffered a stroke and died, about nine years after my father did.

*

My parents were observant Jews, especially during the Jewish holidays. My mother blessed the candles every Friday night. It was a tradition that her family had handed down. They both had very strong family ties. I'm sure when they were youngsters they grew up in a more conservative atmosphere of Judaism; by contrast, we were raised in a pretty liberal manner. First of all, this was a Reform temple here in Muncie, and we had a mixture of people—some from Orthodox backgrounds, some Conservative, and some Reform.

Both of my parents were very active in the temple. My mother was in the sisterhood; my dad was active in the B'nai B'rith. Their social activities were pretty much based around the temple—whatever was going on there during the various holidays: the social events on a Saturday night, social gatherings after temple on Friday nights. I can recall card parties at my parents' house many times with their close friends: the Dobrows, Hazel and Bill Winick—he's Marty Schwartz's uncle—and another couple, the Larry Clines. The Clines and the Winicks and the Dobrows and my folks were all pretty much inseparable.

It was always a battle, of course, to keep the temple going, because we relied on student rabbis from Hebrew Union College. At only one time that I can remember did we have a full-time rabbi here. The younger adults in the community would act as Sunday school teachers. I can remember Mort Pazol teaching Sunday school. I made many good friends—or already had them as friends—when we went to Sunday school, and I was confirmed in the temple. But as far as any real deep religious convictions being taught to us, I don't think that was the case. I can remember sitting in temple as a kid for hours on end, wondering when the services were going to be over.

But the High Holy Days were a very important thing, a very warm thing to me, because it was a family thing. I was talking with an elderly aunt of mine the other day, as a matter of fact—she and her husband are both near ninety years of age—and she said, "I rarely get depressed; it's only during the holidays I get depressed, because there's no more family any more."

The Roth family was very closely knit, and during Passover it was a very big deal that we always had to have the celebration, and the grandparents were there from both sides of the family. I have very fond recollections of those times.

*

When I was a kid in grade school, everybody took Bible study. It was sponsored by the Muncie YMCA. The secretary of the YMCA, a little fellow named H. A. Pettijohn, taught the lessons in school. My parents were a little concerned at first as to whether I should be studying the New Testament. But I always got great marks in it whenever they had the examination, and three years in a row I won a free week at Camp Crosley, the YMCA camp here, and they just thought that was terrific. My folks were so poor at that time that my Uncle George saw to it that if I won the first week, he would pay for the second week—it cost $7 a week at that time.

The Cub Scout program started in Delaware County when I was of Cub Scout age. As a matter of fact, I was the first Scout in Delaware County to go through the Cub Scout program and then become an Eagle Scout. My father was always particularly proud of that fact. In high school I was the first Jewish boy ever invited into The Boys Club, a social club which had been organized by second-generation relatives of the Ball Brothers family. My folks thought that was a wonderful thing, too. I wasn't establishing any new records, but I guess because I wasn't going out and looking for trouble, I was essentially accepted.

*

I do remember one incident with a neighbor boy, a very close friend of mine. When we were in junior high school we got into a spat about something and he called me a dirty Jew. It was the first and only time he ever called me that. I don't think he even knew what it meant; he just got mad because I was getting the best of him. From that time on we were good friends; we never had any more problems about that.

As I reflect back, I think a certain amount of the animosity toward Jews was brought on by action of their own. I think any time a minority group falls under suspicion, the minority reinforces the prejudice by remaining close and intact, I suppose as a matter of self-preservation.

I can think of my Grandmother Schwartz rarely saying anything kind—she was never a particularly kind person; even her compliments about her own family were few and far between. But to her, any non-Jew was *really* an outsider. She had nothing kind to say about them at all. My mother took a little more after my Grandmother Schwartz in that regard. I don't know—maybe they weren't intelligent enough to understand it or to sense it.

I think this was a thorn in my grandfather's side. He was, as I said, well-respected in this community. From the male side of my family—my grandfather and my dad—I suppose I became the kind of person who was not out looking for trouble and didn't run into it to any great extent, as far as anti-Semitism is concerned.

My neighbor down the hall here, Bertha Spurgeon, still talks endearingly of my Grandfather and Grandmother Schwartz.

Her family was well known in the community, and she bought her wedding shoes from my Grandfather Schwartz—and because she did, my grandfather and grandmother were invited to the wedding. Every time I'm with Bertha she talks about my grandfather breaking into tears as she came down the aisle—he was so moved by the whole thing. To this day my Grandfather Schwartz is dearly loved by people in this community. I never heard him talk about being outcasts or about being disliked by the non-Jews.

*

When I was eighteen—the summer between my junior and senior years in high school—I was working as a lifeguard at Touhey Pool.[1] The Delaware Country Club needed a lifeguard, and they came to Touhey Pool and said they wanted a guy to come out and take it over. Three of us were working together at Touhey Pool, but the other two fellows said they weren't interested. So I took the lifeguard's job at Delaware Country Club, even though I knew that no Jews could belong to the club. The chairman of the committee who hired me knew I was Jewish—there was no question about that.

Well, the job turned out to be more than I could handle. They wanted somebody not only to be a lifeguard and give swimming lessons to little kids, but they wanted a pool manager—somebody to run the filtering system and clean the pool, which I knew nothing about. But I stuck it out for the summer.

I had no transportation to and from the club other than my bicycle, so on several occasions my dad dropped me off or picked me up in his car. One day I got a call from the chairman of the committee to see him at his office. He was an attorney here in town and he was very nice to me. He's still here, as a matter of fact, and is very nice to me to this day. He called me in and said, "We've had a complaint, and I would like you to

---

[1] A public swimming pool in Muncie.

straighten it out. It's perfectly all right for your father to come and pick you up at the country club, but I don't want him to get out of his car and wander around as if he's a member." My dad had once gotten out of the car and walked up a few steps to the pool to let me know he was there. He didn't go to the bar; he didn't order a drink; he didn't do anything. But he knew a lot of the people, and somebody had seen him mingling with them and thought he was acting as if he was a member there.

I told the man that I appreciated his telling me and letting me know how he felt, and I said I would tender my resignation.

"Oh, no," he said, "I wouldn't want you to do that."

"I wouldn't have it any other way," I said. "If your ground is too hallowed for my father to walk on, then certainly it's not in keeping with the way I think about things, and I'd much prefer that we don't have any problems in the future. I wouldn't feel comfortable working another day with you." And I quit.

*

My wife and I started dating when I was a sophomore in high school and she was a freshman [1938], believe it or not. Her family had moved here from Toledo when she was thirteen. Her father had been raised in an industrial situation—he had to leave school when he was in the eighth grade to help support his parents and had known nothing in his life except industrial work. With his limited knowledge—and since he was from Toledo, which was also a Ku Klux Klan hotbed—he was not delighted that his daughter was dating a Jew. To this day he is living, and we love each other dearly. He was the first to admit that his anti-Semitism was based upon ignorance. He had never known Jews; all he knew was what he had heard about them, and nothing was ever good.

So Connie and I had some problems when we were dating in high school, but nothing of major consequence. During the war, when I was overseas, we were engaged by proxy. When I came back after the war, her father did stand his ground and said he would not accept Connie's conversion to Judaism. He insisted that he would not see her married in a temple. Our families bent over backwards and tried to figure out how we could work this thing out. My folks bent over farther than he did, I would say: They said if he insisted, we would be married in the Baptist church.

At this point my Uncle George—who had pretty much become the leading factor in our family—intervened. George knew a great deal about the Muncie religious community outside of the Jewish community because he had a fine voice and had sung in several church choirs. Some time back in the 1930s, George actually organized the first Christmas sing in Muncie, which subsequently became the community Christmas sing, a tradition which has stuck for years and years—rather interesting, for a Jew to organize something like this.

In any case, George started calling around and asking if any of the Christian ministers would consider performing a ceremony which would be neutral enough that they wouldn't use the name of Christ. He was turned down a number of times until he called the minister of the Universalist-Unitarian Church here, the Reverend Arthur McDavitt, who said it would be perfectly all right with him: He would do it however we wanted it done. And so we were married—in the Reverend McDavitt's home, actually, which was right next to the church. My father-in-law insisted that those in attendance be limited strictly to family.

So Connie and I used the Universalist-Unitarian Church more or less as a springboard, and when our two kids came along, their Sunday School education was in the Universalist-Unitarian Church. It was quite valuable to them because it taught them to understand other faiths. They're extremely tolerant, very liberal.

After Connie and I were married, we had problems because my parents lived here in town and her parents also lived here in town. My parents wanted to influence us; her parents never really did, but by their silence I think they did. There came a time when it became apparent to me, I think through my wife, that I was going to have to sever the umbilical cord with my family—I had to show my own independence—and that this involved a severance with the temple. And I think, along those lines, I dropped Judaism.

I received some offhanded comment from members of the Jewish community as to why I didn't stick with the temple. We did belong to Green Hills Country Club—that was one thing I *could* do—but it was only a brief exposure. I haven't been active in the Jewish community for a number of years. I am now more or less an outsider.

My daughter is married, has two youngsters and is facing the time now when she's going to have to do something as far as choosing a path for them. Of course, she's half-Jewish and half-Baptist, and she married a non-Jew.

My son is not married. He's in a residency program in medicine. He graduated from medical school last year in Rochester, New York. His religious needs seem to be satisfied in other ways. He's not particularly interested in following any certain line of thinking, as far as religion is concerned.

*

We came back to Muncie in 1948 after I got out of optometry school, and bought a small house. We had no trouble buying that first house, but later we started looking around for a nicer one. We knew that there was a barrier against Jews in Westwood and Kenmore, even though nobody had put it down in writing. I think the Mann addition managed to keep Jews out, too; Mann himself had once drawn up a paper proving that Jews weren't white, or some such thing. But I also knew that Ray Shonfield and his wife owned a lot in Kenmore. I didn't ask Ray why he hadn't built there; I thought maybe he was just waiting until he wanted to.

In any case, I called the realtor who developed Kenmore on the basis that I knew Ray Shonfield owned a lot there but hadn't yet built on it. I told the realtor, "I understand there are some lots available in Kenmore. I'm interested in a lot."

"Well," he said, "at the moment we don't have anything available. But we're going to add a new section to Kenmore, and when that is developed I'll be glad to give you a ring and let you know."

I already knew they were opening a section on the north edge of Kenmore, which I think they wanted to set up sort of as a [Jewish] ghetto. "I don't think I'm interested in your ghetto area," I said.

Later I talked to Ray Shonfield, and he said he'd been told by phone calls on a number of occasions that he'd better not consider building in Kenmore, that his life might not be worth a plugged nickel if he did. Eventually he sold the lot.

But when I grew up as a child, I never felt these terrible restrictions. I never felt put-upon. I felt welcome here. Muncie will always be home to me. I came back when I graduated from school; I came back when I got out of service. Certainly everything has its drawbacks. But in a lot of respects I think we have the best of two worlds in this community. We don't have all the problems of big cities. Certainly we have a lot of advantages that other Jews don't have.

*

In the 1950s, when I was well established, I was approached by two or three members of the board of the Delaware Country Club. They said, "We want to break this barrier (against Jews), and we would like you to join the Delaware Country Club." I was thrilled about the idea and felt honored by it. Maybe I shouldn't have, but I did. Secondarily, I thought it might help the other Jews in the community, because as far as I knew, others had applied for membership, and they had been turned down or not acted upon. Of course that barrier had been the basis for starting the Green Hills Country Club. At this point I didn't belong to Green Hills any longer; I wasn't interested in it.

I told them I'd give it some consideration. I came home and could hardly wait to tell Connie about it. And she said, "I wouldn't give them the satisfaction"—this despite the fact that many of our contemporaries were members of the club. "If you want to join, join," she said. "But I'll never go."

So I told the directors that I didn't think I would join. They said they were very disappointed but they could understand.

Some time later, Sam Dobrow went ahead and joined. And right afterward he said to me, "Why don't you get in?"

"I'll see if I can talk Connie into it," I said.

This time Connie said, "If you want in that badly, let's join." So we did.

FEBRUARY 27, 1979

✵ 6 ✵

"You Were Not Dealing with Urban People"

SAM DOBROW

Sam Dobrow was born in Indianapolis and returned there from Muncie to spend his high school years. In 1938, following his graduation from Indiana University, he settled permanently in Muncie. He has served on the Muncie school board, the Chamber of Commerce, and as president of the Muncie Lions Club and the Green Hills Country Club. Throughout it all his family maintained a rigorously observant Jewish home.

My parents left Russia at a very early age and came to Indianapolis, where they had family. I'm sure it was because of pogroms and to better themselves in this country. My father was a teenager; my mother was a baby. When my parents met they were both living in Indianapolis.

My father took up trade as a tailor and worked for a large tailoring concern in Indianapolis. In the early 1920s a relative had an interest in a scrap business in Muncie and needed somebody to fill in for him. So my father came to Muncie.

In those days the Jewish community of Muncie was a much closer-knit community, but it was a very clique-ish type Jewish community. "Cliques within a clique" is about the way you'd put it. All their activities were in the Jewish community.

They had a social club—probably the Eureka Club, if I recall. I think cards were the main thing that drew them to the club. That was before the temple was built [1922]; afterwards, the temple took over the social area of the community.

I think my father was an active member of the temple. I know in later years his activity was appreciated, because he helped the temple financially a great deal. I think my mother held an office in the sisterhood and Hadassah.

My parents were one of the very few families in Muncie that kept a kosher home. We were one of the very few businesses that closed on the High Holy Days.

*

When I graduated [from Indiana University] in 1938, being an only child I felt an obligation to come to Muncie. I thought the Jewish community was very viable then because everything was centered around the downtown area; they had a lot of Jewish-owned retail stores. The owners were Jewish, the managers were Jewish, and in those days before television the whole social life of the community was there.

The Jews my age did the same things anybody else in their twenties would do. You went out socially like anybody else, and not necessarily within the Jewish community. But I didn't necessarily have more gentile contacts than my parents' generation. In those days at I.U. the gentile sororities would not permit their members to go out with Jewish fellows. And Indiana had a history of anti-Semitism from way back. You were not dealing with urban people; you were talking about more or less small-community people in Indiana. They may not have had connections with the Ku Klux Klan, but at least they were open to it. They probably had it somewhere in their background. And in most cases they were not really familiar with Jews.

I met my wife Frieda in 1942, when I was in the army, stationed at Fort Warren, Wyoming. We were married in 1943. I served in Europe and was discharged in 1946.

*

I really can't recall any specific incidents of anti-Semitism. I think one of the troubles of our people is the fact that if something doesn't go their way, they like an easy excuse, and they can say, "I didn't get the job because this guy was anti-Semitic."

I belong to both the Elks Club and the Delaware Country Club. I was asked to join both of them—actually asked to take the plunge in both instances—the Elks about twenty years ago and the Delaware about twelve. And we were successful in doing it.

As I look back today, first of all, the Jewish community has lost so many members. It is a very small community, and I think, no question about it, living has changed completely for everybody with the advent of television, with the advent of golf courses, tennis courts, and mainly, the generation following my generation don't have the feeling of anti-Semitism, at least not outwardly, when they come in contact with gentiles. I know from my own children that they're part of the group, and people don't think in terms of "He's a Jew, I'm not going to go with him." They think in terms of "They're people and we like their company."

People have become more tolerant because they had to become more tolerant. They're realizing that the world is a smaller place. And there are a lot of fine gentiles who don't approve of anti-Semitism. They take people for what they are, and they realize that if I'm a Jew that's my religion, not my government. As I told someone the other day—we were talking about the Israeli thing—"Just because I'm Jewish doesn't mean I approve of the Israeli view." My country is America. My religion is Jewish. You don't put church and state together. It's not a good idea, and I think a great number of people respect us for it.

The trouble with Jewish communities in larger cities is that they seem to ghettoize themselves. They all live in one area, they all do the same thing, they don't get out of their own sphere. In the small communities, we can't do that. We don't *want* to ghettoize ourselves. The opportunities are better because, I think, our gentile friends have finally found we don't have horns. I think they've found that we are average people and also we're good American citizens.

*

Frieda and I have a similar-type upbringing, and we want to bring our children up the same way. Today we are the only family in Muncie that keeps a kosher home. We are still the only business that closes on the High Holy Days.[1] We come from an observant family, I think *we* are an observant family, and I think this is why our children respect religion: because they were given religion in their home. We didn't wait for a Sunday school teacher or somebody else to teach them; they were taught in the home. They respect their religion; they love us for that.

Our two oldest children live in Muncie; our youngest daughter lives in Chicago, where she and her husband are practicing attorneys. Now I let my children do all the civic activities. It's their time now. They're very active.

*

I think the future in Muncie is good because, fortunately, our family is providing a lot of leadership, and with their background I'm sure there will always be a Jewish community in Muncie. I do think it will be a smaller Jewish community, because there's nothing, really, to bring Jews into a community the size of Muncie. The retail business has changed: They don't have small stores with retail managers any more. The youth don't want to come back to a small town. We have been fortunate that two of our children are living here. The young people are interested in Jewish classes; they're all humanitarians; and they're having children and they're going to raise them as Jews. They might be rather limited, but I think of it as a very live community.

APRIL 30, 1979

---

[1] The Schwartz Paper Co. also closed on the High Holy Days.

7

Avoiding the "Note of Hatred"

ANNA WINICK SCHWARTZ

Born in the Boston area of Lithuanian parents, Anna Schwartz lived in Fort Wayne before coming to Muncie in 1920. She was instrumental in sending her son Martin to Harvard University.

I was born in what I considered Boston. We lived in some of the suburbs—just tiny little places and few Jewish people there. After the Chelsea fire in 1912, in order not to lose too much schooling, I went to live with an aunt in Roxbury.

My father was in Johannesburg, South Africa, teaching for five or seven years before he came to America, while his wife and family were in Boston. He was an ordained rabbi, but I don't recall him ever practicing.

In our family in Boston I had an aunt who had eight sons and was strictly Orthodox. Two of the sons married out of the religion. One son waited [to marry a gentile] until his mother passed on.

I had a sister and brother. My sister died at twenty-one. My brother is dead now too; he was married and had two children, who grew up in Muncie. His son went to Purdue and is in Texas as a business consultant. The daughter has a family in Chicago.

I met my husband in Danville, Illinois. I visited a cousin of mine there. My husband at that time was a traveling sales-man, and of course he called on all the merchants. I met him at my cousin's—I don't recall whether it was in his store or in his home.

We were married in Chicago before we came here.[1] When we came to Muncie my husband's brother had a shoe store; he had been here a good many years.

In Muncie I got myself a job at the [family's] paper com-pany and concentrated on it. My husband was out traveling and I handled the books and paperwork. We worked as a good team.

*

The Ku Klux Klan was very prominent here, so you couldn't help but know and realize it. I had a woman working in the house, just doing ordinary housework. She belonged to it.[2] She was quite thrilled—I think she had to pay $10 to get the sheet—and she wasn't any more aware than that. She evidently didn't detect any difference [between us and gentiles]. She came in and wanted us to know she paid $10 for the sheet. And I said, "Fine." Why argue with the woman? She's already made a purchase; she wanted to belong to the group; and I let it go.

But we had to be careful with the children that we didn't get any bitterness in their feeling and feel that they're going to fight for their rights. So in our home we handled it—I don't know about the others [Jews], but as far as my husband and I, we handled it very carefully. Whatever we told the children, we taught them for the interest of all concerned.

---

[1] The Schwartzes moved from Chicago to Fort Wayne and then to Muncie.
[2] Presumably she had joined the Kamelias, women's auxiliary of the Ku Klux Klan.

*

I belonged to the temple sisterhood I guess as long as I've been in Muncie. The temple was always in need of a little help, but it was done quietly. Our purpose was to keep the community together and not to have the youngsters feel that they're out of contact with each other. And yet we were very careful not to get the note of hatred in our Jewish children. We felt they'd get along so much better at school and all if they knew this, because they could learn by observing. It would have been unfair to the Jewish children to feel that they're different.

We celebrated the High Holidays, we observed all we could at home—quietly and without making a fuss about it. And we explained to the children what the celebration was about, and they learned it that way.

*

I think Jewish people will always try to give the best training and advantages to their children. When our children went to school they had to concentrate on schooling, and naturally they had to have some goal. "Where are we going [to college]? Where do we want to go?" So Marty went to Harvard.

I don't think Marty was very happy about having to go into commerce [in the family's wholesale paper business]. I think he would have much preferred to continue studying, increasing his knowledge of the world we're living in. But then one has to get by. It takes clothes and it takes a lot of things.

*

A lot of Jews are moving out of Muncie, and I'm commencing to think that they're probably right. They want to give the children a little more Jewish upbringing.

APRIL 4, 1979

❧ 8 ❧

"You Can't Be Anonymous"

MARTIN D. SCHWARTZ

Martin Schwartz, a Harvard graduate and second-generation Muncie paper merchant, was among the first Jews accepted into Muncie's prominent civic and social organizations.

I was born in Fort Wayne, Indiana, on March 27, 1917. As I understand it, the family name in Lithuania was Charny, taken from the Russian word "black." My father, Leo, was the youngest of seven brothers, and when the oldest brother came to this country, between 1890 and 1900, he decided that the name "Charny" was inappropriate for a person of his stature, and that the name "Schwartz," which was the German version, was much more dignified. At that time Germany was certainly considered the most progressive country in Europe, intellectually, economically, and socially. That's why he took the name.

Two brothers followed him. Maurice, who eventually ended up in Muncie, took the name "Schwartz" in the same way. My father, the next to arrive, did what he was told to do: I have his naturalization papers, and he was naturalized as Leo Schwartz.

My father's father in Lithuania was sort of a general merchant, particularly in lumber. On my father's side the family has been traced back to 1492. Most of the Jews expelled from Spain that year migrated either up to Italy or out to Holland, and then moved up through Austria, Poland, or Lithuania.

My father's mother came from a family named Grabowski that came to Philadelphia and went into the cigar business; they are the original developers of El Producto cigars.

My father came to America in 1903, probably to avoid service in the Russian Army. He was naturalized in 1912. He was fairly well educated for a Jewish boy at that time. He had been sent to a school in the port city of Libau, Latvia. That was some sort of special deal for him, so his family must have had some sort of influence or money. I remember as a kid, when we lived on Charles Street [in Muncie, after 1924], he had some kind of school uniform in a trunk upstairs, with a high-buttoned kind of tunic, sort of like you'd see Stalin wearing.

He was quite literate. He spoke Russian, but the language they all spoke was Yiddish. He was very good in Hebrew and pretty good in German. I don't know if he had any English before he left Europe, but his English was excellent when I knew him. He was an avid reader and a great talker. His skills were primarily a sharp mind, a good wit, and a fine personality, so he came over here and started selling for his brother Maurice, who at that time had a plant in Matthews, Indiana,[1] making glass [lamp] chimneys. My father never had any help from any immigrant agency coming over, since he had these two well-established brothers. He was something of a dandy all his life—something of a "dresser."

My mother's father was a rabbi, David Winick. He must have been someone of academic or intellectual stature, because in his little area of Lithuania he was chosen by the Jews to represent them directly at the Tsar's court. But these are hearsay kind of stories that I have been unable to verify. My grand-

---

[1] A village of about 750 people twenty miles northwest of Muncie.

mother [his wife] died in childbirth in her early thirties. After the death of his wife my grandfather went to South Africa during the gold rush there [1895]. He must have died young, around the age of forty. I have heard somewhere that he had remarried. Something must have gone on, because he was not buried in consecrated ground in a Jewish cemetery where his first wife—my grandmother—was buried. There obviously was some breach of Orthodox law.

My mother and my uncle were brought up as orphans by relatives in the Boston area.

My father married my mother in 1915. They were introduced in Danville, Illinois, through relatives. By that time he was a traveling salesman for a paper company in Fort Wayne. With the coming of electricity, gas mantels and glass chimneys immediately died out, and then the glass plant folded in Matthews. My uncle Maurice [Schwartz] came to Muncie and opened up a clothing store called Moxie's on Walnut Street between Adams and Jackson. It was named after the soft drink, but it fit him, too. He was a man of talent, colorful, a good gambler and a great card player. Before he opened his glass factory he was with the famous Tex Rickard, the fight promoter, in the Yukon Gold Rush. Ultimately at the beginning of the Depression [of the 1930s] he left Muncie because of debts. He moved to New York, opened up a dry cleaning establishment, and had a son and daughter. His son Jimmy developed a process for re-doing suede and leather and then was killed right before World War II in an automobile accident. Jimmy's sister Marjorie is still there,[2] and her husband has been running the business ever since. It's now called Leathercraft Process of America, and they do suede cleaning and dying and get business from all over the world.

---

[2] Marjorie died subsequently.

By the way, they changed their name back to Charny when they went to New York. By the 1930s, you see, "Charny" sounded infinitely more elegant than "Schwartz" did, which shows there are styles in names, too.

So after the glass plant in Matthews closed, my father had to find work elsewhere. He found a job with the old Rothschild Brothers Paper Company in Fort Wayne. This wasn't the famous Rothschild family. These Rothschilds were Joe and Otto, two bachelor brothers who happened to be Jewish. Apparently they were quite well-to-do; I believe they owned a lot of stock in the General Telephone Company that was just getting under way up there. They ran this wholesale paper company in Fort Wayne, which was subsequently bought out by the competitive company, Fisher Brothers, which is still there.

*

After my father and mother were married they came back to Fort Wayne, where he had a job as a salesman. I remember my mother telling me he made all of $30 a month. In those days his territory was determined by the railroads and where they went out of Fort Wayne. So he had long trips, which I remember as a kid and which continued after we started in business here. He was always on the old Nickel Plate as far east as Cleveland, and then he would go up the whole Ohio territory, which he called his "golden territory." That's where he established himself best. His customers were primarily grocery stores. He was selling all kinds of things [for Rothschild Brothers]—toilet paper, paper towels—but he also sold washboards, clotheslines, clothespins, jar rings. We [Schwartzes] call ourselves paper people, but there have always been a lot of things that have nothing to do with paper.

I was born in 1917 and they moved to Muncie in 1920. I often asked him: Why Muncie? He said he had concepts of the kind of business he wanted to run, and that would be where he would tell his customers what they were going to get. He said when he worked for Rothschild Brothers, he never knew what they were going to ship. He was a typical salesperson in the sense that he thought he could do a better job than the management could.

The Schwartz Paper Company was begun in December 1920 in a two-story brick building down on 628 South Walnut Street that my mother and father paid $12,500 for. It's still standing; we still use it as a warehouse. They bought it from Miller Brewing Company of Milwaukee, because that was the beginning of prohibition and all of these brewers around the country owned the real estate for their saloons.

*

Muncie had a pretty active Jewish community in those days. Our temple was dedicated in 1922, and believe it or not I remember that building when it was going up. Since its inception in about 1875 the congregation has always been affiliated with the Union of American Hebrew Congregations—that's the Reform branch [of Judaism]. And this [the 1920s] was the period we call "The Period of Classic Reform." Most of the Jews in Muncie attended that temple, but there were always a few unrelenting Orthodox who would never set foot in it.

When we first came to Muncie I would say most of the Jews were in the clothing business. There was a Morris Shapiro from Chicago, who had a clothing manufacturing company called Victor Garment Company, upstairs on the corner of Howard and Walnut. He may have come to Muncie because of cheap labor. Some of the other Jews were in the scrap business. When my father started the wholesale paper business, that was a little odd. The retail clothing merchants on Walnut Street eventually died out and their stores were sold or went out of business. Or if they made it well enough economically, they simply moved away to more acceptable climates.

I've never thought much about the Jewish interest in clothing, but my quick response would be that a lot of these Jews who came through this part of the country came as peddlers, either with a pack on their back or with a horse and wagon. They had to carry things that were transportable and didn't need a lot of special care. I know that a lot of the well-known department stores in this country started from Jewish peddlers. Around here I think of Weiler Brothers in Portland [Ind.].[3] Now the grandson, young Ray, has a Weiler's in Anderson.[4] But I remember the old man [Weiler] up there [in Portland]. Right around the 1920s he was riding in a chauffeured car. They had come from Germany. So a lot of these people who may have started out with a little bit of money went to these small towns in the Middle West and opened up. I think that was probably the easiest thing for them to do—to open up clothing stores and then branch out into other departments.

The only [Jewish] people who leave [Muncie] leave because they want to go to another Jewish community. Many of them may have been very lonely here. Being a Jew in Muncie, Indiana, you can't be anonymous. And I think a lot of them feel uncomfortable in the sort of showcase, if you want to call it that, of Muncie, as Jews. And they would have found Muncie completely untenable if they're Orthodox.

*

A lot of them [Jewish merchants] went out of business during the Depression. I know that we had a great struggle in my family. It's interesting, though, that from the beginning we had the aura of having money, even when we didn't. I've never quite understood that. We didn't have any money, really, until after the Depression.

My father started with total capital of $4,000, most of which my mother had saved. She never spent any money; she was the money-grubber in the family. She was an extremely frugal person who never had anything, and poverty was always part of her life. In later years she told me, "You know, you and I have had different backgrounds. I understand that money will never mean to you what it has meant to me, because you were never in the kinds of positions that I was in." The money meant

_____

[3] A county seat town of 7,000, thirty miles northeast of Muncie.
[4] A city of 50,000, twenty miles southwest of Muncie.

security to her that she never had as a child. She's often told
me how she cried when she got out of the sixth grade because
she knew her aunts and cousins were not going to let her go to
school any more; she had to go to work. I think that's one of
the great reasons she wanted to see me well educated, in a
prestigious place.

*

I remember when I was a kid I used to play with a young
fellow named Bob Norcross, whose father was one of the big
wheels of the Klan in Muncie, and Sparky Walsh, who is a
good Catholic, and Freddie McClellan. There was a whole
group of us, and we didn't make much distinction [among
ourselves]. But we knew what was going on and who was supposed to be for and against various things. But it was never
very serious to us as kids. We used to talk about going down
on East Washington Street into a big house with big pillars in
front of it that was the Klan headquarters. They had the spare
sheets up there and everything. We used to go upstairs on the
third floor where they had all the Klan sheets lined up, and all
the kids used to dress up in those and play upstairs. This may
have been '27 or '28.[5]

I remember the Klan parades down on Walnut Street. Many
of them. My father used to take me down there, and I'd sit on
his shoulders, because I was a little kid. They were more specifically anti-Catholic and anti-black. There weren't enough
Jews, you see, around Muncie to make much of a target. Most
of the Jews were in the retail business on Walnut Street, but
most of them had very good relationships with their clientele,
and I don't think anybody had any great hostilities to them as
business people.

But I remember some of those Klan torchlight parades. You
know, their idea of Americanism was to have a big fat gal seated

---

[5]   When Schwartz was about ten years old.

on a white draft horse with the American flag draped over its rump. In retrospect I never felt it was a threat to my parents; if that had been the case I don't think we'd have gone. They would knock blacks off the street or push them aside, because they were always hooded and nobody knew who was doing it.

Membership in the Klan was a very hush-hush thing, but I knew who some of the people were by word of mouth. I remember in the 1930s Pete Jolley, the basketball coach and history teacher [at Muncie High School, now Central High], was from New Castle,[6] and he used to say, "Well, you know, everybody joined; all you needed was $10 or $15 for your sheet, and it was considered *the* thing to do." He said he was just a youngster when he joined. He said they were out for his $10, and he was laughing about it because he didn't consider it a matter of any particular significance.

It was not the kind of racism that I have read about in the South. I have the impression that many of the people, frankly, were really kind of dumb bunnies who didn't know what they were doing; it was a sort of camaraderie and dress-up kind of thing. The rank-and-file weren't playing for keeps; the officers and managers were. They got a commission on membership and everything else. It was damn good business.

*

I remember as a kid my parents being horrified and talking a great deal about the Leopold-Loeb [murder] case in Chicago [1924]. They were very much concerned in those days. Their whole emphasis was that we were our brothers' keepers. It was a serious concern in our household. It was a heinous crime, no question about it, but my parents were primarily concerned because all three—the victim and the two perpetrators—were Jews from very prominent homes in Chicago.

---

[6] A city of 21,000 about twenty miles south of Muncie.

*

My parents didn't have a great deal of social life. Theirs was more generally concerned with getting ahead in business. My mother worked from the day the company opened. She was inside and my father was outside. He was the seller, the personality, the guy who made it go. But she was the one who sat on the purse and kept the books.

Occasionally they would have somebody in for dinner. Maybe a rabbi. My father was a great one for anyone who had any Jewish learning. But in those days there were an awful lot of phonies—so-called rabbis and people soliciting money for various institutions. He could spot them, because he was a good Hebrew scholar. When they'd come in and start talking to him in Yiddish, he could go either way in two different languages. He would immediately start to quiz them, and he would tell me, "This one is a phony."

My mother's working in the business was atypical among Jewish women in Muncie. A lot of the Jewish social life in those days revolved around what they called the Eureka Club, which was on the second floor of a building on Main Street. The first services and the first religious school I ever went to in this town were on that second floor. The community kept that long after the temple was built, primarily as a place for social gatherings—poker, mah jongg, and pinochle.

I would not have called my family religious. We observed the major Jewish holidays. My father was well-steeped in this but was not particularly observant. We didn't keep kosher. His main observances were the *yahrzeit* or the anniversaries of the deaths of his parents. Of course on High Holy days and Passover we would always be in the temple. And we were members of the temple from the beginning.

I would say that our home values were basically middle-class American—the great stress put upon the virtue of thrift, of work, of learning. That may or may not have been a middle-class value; maybe that was where the Jewish value came in. There was a lot of emphasis on body cleanliness, mental cleanliness. A lot of this, I suppose, if I think about it, would have been Protestant or Puritan. But there was an enormous emphasis in my family on personal integrity—that you don't lie, that you are morally straight. The kind of things that H. A. Pettijohn used to teach us at the [Muncie] YMCA.

My parents were capitalists *par excellence* before they knew what the word was. Having left Lithuania to come here for freedom, my father was very hostile to that whole Bolshevik business. As I have reconstructed it, my father came out of that same kind of intellectual background of people like Ben Gurion from the 1880s on. He told me that as a boy he'd have to go to the outhouse back of their home to read a modern Russian novelist like Chekhov or Turgenev—his father would have knocked him over if he found him, because he said a Jewish boy of his caliber should always study the Torah. My father was a rebel in that sense. He loved poetry and used to recite it by the hour. But socialism—no!

*

The temple was the center of the Jewish community and social life—that was typical all over the country in those periods—so it was almost a necessity if you wished to be identified. Now, there were individuals in this community who were never members of the temple—for example, Max Zeigler, who helped many factories and businesses get started here. There are great stories about Max Zeigler, but he was always an outsider. Or a guy like Sam Gold, who in the early days had a second-hand store down on South Walnut. He was not a member of the temple in the early days.

When I was a boy there was always some kind of religious school going on, but that was never terribly effective in my day, or in my children's day. Whatever went on at the temple, we were there. Whatever was available, we did. But the Sunday school was never a highly organized congregational effort because we never had a permanent rabbi. Intermittently we had a regular rabbi who would conduct the religious school.

I've often asked my father why he didn't teach me Hebrew. His attitude was, "What the devil would you need this for in America? What would you do with it?" He was intellectually inclined, but he was unable to see the relevance of learning Hebrew for a young boy in America at that time. I've often felt that was something I would have liked to have had, and I've been working on it a little late in life.

My father did perform my *bar mitzvah*, taught me everything. But of course I learned the Hebrew sections by rote. I didn't know the language, so I had it in my ear. I've had it in my ear all these years.

*

Going to Harvard never occurred to me until about the end of my junior year [of high school]. My father had a stroke and relatives of ours from Boston came out. The father had gone to Harvard. He was a poor immigrant boy from Boston, and his son was already in Harvard. The son was about three years older than I, and they began talking it up and pointing out that coming from Muncie it would be a very easy thing for me to get in. And they were right. In those days, Harvard had an admissions program by which they would admit you if you were in the highest one-seventh of the boys in your graduating high school class. That's the only reason I got in. I couldn't have passed the College Boards in those days.

In high school my being Jewish was never a problem. I was asked into the Triangle Club very early in the game, and that was a big part of my high school life. Then I ended up my senior year as president. In fact, I suppose that all through high school and college and since, I have used my Judaism not as a halter but as a point of departure. Harvard was very traumatic for me the first year. The first day I got there I was told by a Jewish fellow all the things I could or couldn't do because I was Jewish. My first response was: "I'm in the wrong place; I'd better go back to Muncie."

I never remember any discussions about what I would do when I got out of Harvard. I think it was just an assumption on everybody's part that I would go into the paper business. That was the way I read it, and of course my father was sick; that made it even more imperative. Otherwise I probably would have opted for a life in academe, at least at the outset. If I knew all the things I know now about academe, I doubt it.

*

I went out with Christian girls all through high school, but it was understood when I was young that I would never look to any of them as a marriage partner. It never occurred to me that I would not marry a Jewish girl. That's a little shocking when I think of my children.

I married a Jewish girl named Helen Berger, whom I met in New York after college, and we are still married. Her father was born in Indianapolis, of Hungarian descent. Helen's mother was born in Austria-Hungary.

Nobody arranged our marriage—that was another generation. After all, Helen went to Wellesley and I was at Harvard, and we were completely absorbed in the American romantic ideal: Nobody was going to make any selections for *us*. But it was just as clear to her that she would only marry a Jewish fellow. That just never was an issue. My sister also married a Jewish guy who was here at Ball State during World War II.

I remember [Jewish] people moving to Muncie in the '20s who were already intermarried. That was a source of great consternation and shock, although of course it had no particular bearing on me. The first was a fellow named Harry Ritoff. He had a retail store and was married to a beautiful blonde woman who was not Jewish. I remember his mother used to cry to my parents about Harry's marrying out of the faith. That became much more common after World War II. I have seen many of the old prejudices break down since the World War II era, and as a result I think the children who grew up in this era didn't feel the kinds of affinity for the old religious and ethnic and social ties that I felt in my generation. I certainly know that my children don't seem to have that feeling—and I think we do more religious observing in our home than my parents did.

We have many intermarriages in our little Jewish community now in which the wife who is not born Jewish becomes very active in the [Jewish] community. When Jewish women marry gentiles, I don't notice as much conversion among the males. But I'm skeptical about the conversions to Judaism I have seen, both male and female, because I've seen this great passionate attachment to a new religion, and then it peters out in a year or two. I don't see any real continuity except when there's a marriage.

*

I did not realize how much the Jewish community was isolated in the '20s and '30s from the mainstream of the establishment. Jews had been much more active at the turn of the century than they subsequently were. World War I, apparently, unleashed all kinds of prejudice in this country that hadn't been overt beforehand. Jews had been members of the Elks; my father was an Elk. He had been into the Masonic Lodges and everything back around 1900 to 1910. Then the restrictions began to come in, and it became very difficult if not impossible for Jews to enter into some of these things.

A lot of these restrictions were established by a group of the 1920s and '30s establishment in Muncie. They were never quite sure *why* they were prejudiced, but this was common in a lot of the things going on in this country.

Unfortunately, there was never a Jewish member of a service club in Muncie until the middle 1960s. And Jews didn't make an effort to join. Of course during the '20s you had the problem of the Klan, and Jewish business people particularly tried to keep a low profile on the grounds that most of their customers were Klansmen.

I was the first [to break] that barrier. I was in Kiwanis first, but frankly I was not interested in what went on there, so I dropped out. Then later I was asked into Rotary. Of course I had gone into the Masonic Orders after World War II. I didn't have too much trouble with that, but I was the first Jew who had gone in in about twenty years. And then, of course, came the Delaware Country Club. I was not the first Jew there; I was about the second or third. And then, of course, the Muncie Club. They never had any Jewish members; I was the first one there. But all of these things I've kind of taken "tongue in cheek," you know. I thought: "Now they've got their house Jew." You know what I mean?

The only Jew I can think of in any political position in Muncie was Charles Indorf, who was the commissioner of public works under the George Dale administration [1931–35]. And Charley was absolutely untouchable morally; he was too straight to ever take a nickel. And he was known that way in this community. He was an immigrant, spoke with an accent, and I remember he used to go up and tell people to put salt up around the sidewalks where the grass was growing in the cracks, because there wasn't any money for doing it. He took his job seriously. He was a civil servant in the best sense of the word.

*

The main problem with anti-Semitism in this town was where you could live. That was the most overt and clearly restrictive kind of policy. You know, if you can pay your bills, people overlook a lot of things. But we could not buy a home in Westwood, and then when Charley Bender opened Kenmore it was the same thing. It wasn't directed against anybody as an individual—it was just because you were a Jew.

There wasn't a specific Jewish neighborhood in Muncie, but in my day most of the Jews lived within walking distance of the temple on Jackson Street, even though they weren't Orthodox. It was just the community pattern. The 1920s were the days of streetcars. When the automobile started to become plentiful in the 1920s, our family got a Model T [Ford]. But until then my father had done all his traveling by railroad and by interurban. Everybody who could lived as close to downtown as possible, so you could walk downtown. There were never enough Jews to make an enclave, but I would say they all lived within maybe a twenty-square-block area. Before World War I most of them lived on the east side of town. And then, of course, the whole community moved west.

I've been active in all kinds of things for many years. I served in World War II and stayed in the reserves until 1970. After World War II I was president of the Muncie Civic Theatre, and I was on the Red Cross board at one time. I filled an unexpired term for somebody on the Chamber of Commerce. As for Jewish organizations, I helped develop the Harvard Center for Jewish Studies. I'm now an overseer for Hebrew Union College—they're trying to raise money, so I accepted that with the full understanding that I'm not going to get into the fundraising business. I'm not particularly interested in the fundrising aspects, although you can't really get into any voluntary organization today without taking some look at it.

*

I have four daughters, ranging in age from thirty-six to Joanie, who will be twenty in August. All of them are college graduates, and the two eldest have master's degrees. The oldest, Judy, went to Wheaton College in Massachusetts and Tufts for her master's. She married a fellow named Andrew D. Ball, who happens to be Jewish, although he never had as much Jewish background as Judy did. They have two boys; both of them are in Jewish religious schools on Saturday and Sunday. They seem to be interested in Jewish things, although they live in the Washington, D.C. area, so they have a lot more facilities. Judy is a career person; she is full-time with the American Association of University Women.

Susie lives in Dayton, Ohio, where she's been teaching school for the last four or five years. She married a very nice Jewish fellow and has two children, a girl and a boy, seven and four. But she got divorced last year or the year before. The seven-year-old is in the Hillel Academy, a Jewish parochial school. Susie didn't feel the Dayton public school system was good enough; she wanted a private school, and that happened to be about the best private school she could find.

Debby, my third daughter, also graduated from Wheaton and then decided to seek the simple life and went out to Lander, Wyoming,[7] which happened to be the base for the National Outdoor Leadership School. They do mountaineering and other things, in order to learn life in the rough. She didn't complete that course—she got hurt in the first five days—and she met this young man there. She came back East for a year, worked in Stowe, Vermont, as a ski bum one winter, and then went back out to Lander and married this guy, who is not Jewish. She's been working ever since she's been there; she's very competent. She worked first in a bank, and now she's working for the hospital as the credit manager. They were apparently surprised to find someone of her background. They're offering her all kinds of incentives to keep her happy.

I think there is a thread in all my daughters: They're all strong individuals and doing their own thing, whatever it may be.

*

I don't sense the kind of commitment [to Judaism] in some of the younger people that I think we had. But we had other pressures keeping us committed, like anti-Semitism. If I understand anything about Jewish history, these periods have come many times: We become fat and complacent, and then a big whack of anti-Semitism always brings us back. Now, I'm not looking for that, but we have lived through the worst in the history of the world, and I have a feeling there will always be what we call the "saving remnant"—a small segment of people devoted to the philosophical, the theological, the moral values of this tradition. This is the position I'm at in my life now. This is not where I was as a younger man. In fact, as a young man I questioned very seriously what those values were and why they would be worth preserving.

---

[7] A town of about 8,000.

*

My wife and I made a decision a long time ago. We've been fortunate enough; we've done a lot of traveling and we've seen a great deal of the world. We have looked around the world for retirement places or second homes, and we made a decision about ten years ago that we would finish our lives in Muncie. Or at least this is where we're going to call "home."

And it's for a very simple reason: Here we are known. We know the people and the place. Very simply, we have status. Let's not kid ourselves. If you go to Florida or Timbuktu or any place, you're just another old has-been retiree looking for something to do. This is my home. This is where I feel most comfortable. This is where I know my way around and where, at least, I don't have to explain who I am or what I am. Everybody here knows who and what I am.

April 4, 1979

The Moses Cohen family, 1904. Left to right: Bess (16); Moses (47); Daniel (22); Benjamin (10); Pearl (12); Sarah (40); and Frank (20). The Cohens were pioneers in the scrap business.

The Herschel Ringold family, 1904. Above, left to right: Lena, Sam, and Sarah (Mrs. Moses Cohen). Below, left to right, Anna, Reva, and Herschel. The Ringolds followed the Cohens to Muncie in the 1880s.

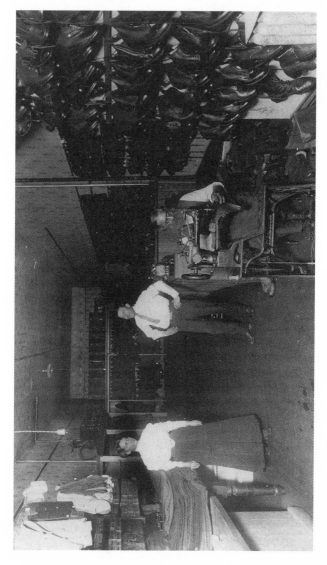

Sadie and Sam Gold in their South Walnut Street clothing store. The cobbler can be identified only as "Jake."

Sadie Gold and daughters Ida and Edith on vacation in northern Indiana, about 1918.

Sisters Ida and Edith Gold, about 1920.

The office of the Schwartz Paper Company, 628 South Walnut Street about 1923. At left is bookkeeper Herb Murray; seated is receptionist Bernice Greenlee; standing, left to right, are Anna Schwartz, Leo Schwartz, and Anna's brother, William Winick. The latter three co-founded the business in 1921.

The two lives of Ray Shonfield: in the 1920s, second from right, as a young saxophone player in Riley's jazz band, Muncie; after 1930, proprietor of Shonfield's Clothing Store on West Main Street.

The elegant Hotel Roberts, Corner of High and Howard, Muncie. George Roberts, a Polish Jew, made a fortune during the natural gas boom in east central Indiana before building the hotel, completed in 1922 and now the Radisson-Roberts.

At Muncie's original airport on South Hackley, a crowd gathers in the summer of 1929 to see the Nekoosa-Edwards Paper Co.'s Ford Trimotor, down from Port Edwards, Wisc. Standing under the plane's nose are Leo Schwartz (in shirtsleeves), daughter Elaine, and son Marty. It was Marty's first ride in a plane, and he recalls that it had wicker seats.

Wedding photo of Ida and Archie Lapin,
October 19, 1930, Hotel Roberts, Muncie.

The Why, owned by Will and Pearl Freund, 523 South Walnut—a clothing store for workingmen in "the 'red light district' of Muncie," according to their son, Bernard.

The 11-year-old Morton (Bud) Roth in 1934, with his grandparents, Sam and Fannie Schwartz, and his sisters, Shirley (left) and Marilyn (center).

The twenty-year-old Morton (Bud) Roth in 1943, when he was serving in Texas in the U.S. Army Air Corps.

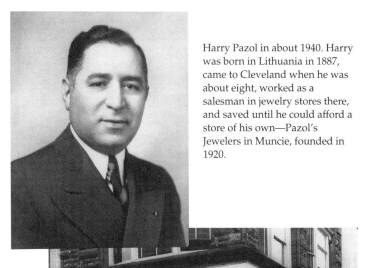

Harry Pazol in about 1940. Harry was born in Lithuania in 1887, came to Cleveland when he was about eight, worked as a salesman in jewelry stores there, and saved until he could afford a store of his own—Pazol's Jewelers in Muncie, founded in 1920.

Pazol's Jewelers, one of the last Jewish-owned family businesses along Walnut Street, as it looked in 1941.

Mort Pazol in 1934. After World War II, Mort and his brother, Herb, took over the jewelry store when their father moved to Los Angeles.

Confirmation Class, June 1932, Temple Beth El, Muncie. Rabbi Hirsch Freund is in the front row, center. Others in the front row include Ann Kallmeyer's cousin, Peggy Marx (far left), and Roberta Zaltsberg (second from left), who later married Joe Freadlin. In the back row, second from left, A. C. Bernstein; fourth from right, Robert Burgauer; far right, Herbert Pazol.

Bar mitzvah, June 1954: Rabbi Maurice Feuer and Lawrence Pazol, nephew of Mort Pazol.

Temple Beth El, corner of Jackson and Council, Muncie, dedicated in 1922.

Martin D. Schwartz and his mother, Anna Winick Schwartz, in a snapshot from 1936 (taken in Cambridge, Massachusetts, during the Harvard Tercentenary); and in a portrait from the 1970s.

Ida and Archie Lapin on their fiftieth wedding anniversary.

❋ 9 ❋

The Gentile Wife

BEULAH LAZAR

After marrying into a Jewish family in 1952, Beulah Lazar maintained her association with the Presbyterian Church while her husband kept his membership in Temple Beth El. But she joined the temple's sisterhood and Hadassah, worked as a secretary at the temple's Sunday school, and agreed to raise their children as Jews. She remained involved in the temple after her husband, Rudy Lazar, died in 1967. At the time of this interview she was a secretary at the Emerson School in Muncie.

I grew up in a little town in Oklahoma called Grainola.[1] I lived all my life and graduated from high school there, and I never really thought of going to college because my family was poor, as most of them were in that town. So the idea was just to get out and get a job. I got a job in Wichita, but I had a cousin in Muncie named Eleanor Smith, a well-to-do spinster. I had known her only through letters. She had written and

---

[1] A village near the Oklahoma-Kansas state line, population seventy-nine in 1950.

asked me if I would like to come to Muncie and go to business college, and I came with the idea of staying six months. Well, I came the day before World War II started [December 1941].

She and I got along very well, and after I got out of business college I took a job at what was then called the Merchants Trust Company,[2] and I stayed. That's really how I met Rudy, my husband. I had never really known any Jewish people until I met Rudy and became acquainted with him and his family, and through him of course I met other people in the community.

Rudy was born in Chicago. His father came there as a young man after running away from the Russian army; his mother came from England. They had a grocery store in Chicago; I remember Rudy telling me they were one of the first Jewish families to move into a gentile neighborhood. Rudy's father died in 1941, so I never knew him.

Rudy's mother came to live here with her brother, Harry Graff, who owned Bert's Ladies Ready-to-Wear store. Mr. Graff was getting up in years and needed somebody to manage the store. When Rudy came out of service after World War II, he had been in college at Loyola University in Chicago. He didn't know what he wanted to do, so his Uncle Harry made him the offer to come here and manage the store. He decided to try it, and he loved it and stayed until the store closed.

He learned the business from the ground up from his uncle, who had been in the clothing business all his life. His uncle came to this country as a young man and went to work at sewing in the garment district in New York. Then he opened up a manufacturing business in Chicago. So Rudy had the opportunity to learn all about the clothing business from his uncle. He went to Chicago and New York on buying trips; he liked the challenge, he liked being in business, he liked being down-

---

[2] Subsequently American National Bank.

town with the other businessmen, and so I think he really enjoyed the community.

Rudy was not a joiner, really. He belonged to B'nai B'rith, which was part of the temple, although I think it was because they got to play cards after they ate. Then he was one of the charter members of the Green Hills Country Club. It was started by Morton Standt and Burle Plank, and most of the people of the Jewish community did belong. We had an awfully good time when we went out there, because everybody knew everyone. Of course, they had never been able to belong to a country club here in Muncie, because the Delaware [Country Club] didn't admit Jews at that time. So this was something for them—to be able to have a country club and to play golf. Rudy had never played golf, but he learned after the club opened up.

*

I remember once when Rudy and I were still dating, we went into the Hotel Roberts and were sitting in the bar. We may have been eating—I can't remember now. I was so embarrassed because the people behind us were saying anti-Semitic things. I really wanted to get up and leave, but I don't know whether it bothered Rudy or not.

My own experience [as a Jewish wife in a predominantly gentile city] has been very enjoyable. I suppose it's one reason I have remained active in the sisterhood, because it's really the only contact that I have with the Jewish community. I have felt sometimes that when they talk about anti-Semitism *they* have prejudice also, maybe with good reason. There have been times when I have wanted to say something, but I would hold my tongue.

I've always belonged to the sisterhood at the temple and been active most of the time, going to the monthly meetings. This is the first time I've been an officer. They asked me to be the treasurer, and I accepted. I've always belonged to Hadassah. Of course I'm not a member of the temple; my affiliation is with the Presbyterian Church. However, I do go to temple services occasionally—I was just there last night, in fact.

All my other interests are the church, and I've always liked music. I belong to the women's church circle.

*

I wouldn't say religion played a real big part in our home. We were each going our own way, although I always attended temple with Rudy, mostly on Yom Kippur and Rosh Hashanah. When he went to temple I always attended with him. But he never attended church with me—I don't know that I ever really invited him. I think I was trying to be fair to him and also fair to myself. It's maybe sticky sometimes.

It was my decision that the children should be brought up in the Jewish religion, and of course I always felt that our home would be known as a Jewish home and that the children would be known as Jews, and I still think they consider themselves Jews. However, they are not active. They don't go to temple, and most of the time never even go on the High Holy Days, which really distresses me. I would like them to be active at least to the point where they would go once a year or have some contact. By my not being Jewish, I think they don't really feel their Jewishness. Also, they were the only Jewish children going to Emerson School, and the only Jewish children at Muncie Central High School most of the time. We haven't lived in a Jewish neighborhood. In through Halteman Village you find more Jewish families. But they are scattered all over the city.

I was always glad when the holidays were over, whether they were Easter or the Jewish holidays or Christmas. Christmas I always played down in my home because I could never celebrate it as I wanted to. Out of respect for Rudy, we always called it "my Christmas tree," although he always enjoyed it. I never got much help from him with Christmas shopping. But then, his store was open late from Thanksgiving until Christmas, so he was very tired and worn out with just his business. But at the last minute he would always want to know what I had gotten certain ones for Christmas presents, and then he'd decide it wasn't enough, so he'd get me to go out and do more last-minute Christmas shopping. But it was always sort of a relief to me when the holidays were over.

There was not too much emphasis on Hanukah in our home—more after the children were in Sunday school, of course. And when I was working with the Sunday school I'd try to emphasize it more. Their formal Jewish education was limited to Sunday school, and the two younger ones rebelled, so they didn't even get through religious school. The last year I was the secretary there, and oftentimes they just refused to go. So I said, "Well, this isn't doing me any good, and it isn't doing you any good," so we gave up on it.

*

Most of Rudy's close friends were Jewish. His gin rummy games were with Jewish friends, sometimes at individual homes but most of the time out at Green Hills Country Club. There was a foursome, and then a lot of times the men would get together in someone's home and they would have a gin rummy game. I really can't think of any close friends he had who were not Jewish.

*

I think there will always be a Jewish community here. It's getting harder all the time to run the temple. I constantly hear about money problems that they have. So many moneyed people are retired and living in Florida. The people who are left are the young people starting out and the college profes-sors. They're not poverty-stricken, but they don't have the great sums of money to give that some of your merchants had at one time. At the time I was married we had a full-time rabbi here. Of course they can no longer afford a full-time rabbi.

Any organization is just as strong as its members. In our church it shouldn't depend on the minister to hold a church together. If you have dedicated members, you'll always have some sort of service. This year they don't have a rabbi every week, but they have lay services, and the ones I've attended have been very good. We have about the same number that come for lay services as when the rabbi comes. The average

Friday night attendance is twenty to twenty-five people. But then there's not a very large Jewish community, either. At the Passover dinner this week we were supposed to have eighty-two people. For one reason or another we didn't have that many.

*

I've been very happy to be a part of the Jewish community. I've enjoyed it. I feel that I have grown by knowing the Jewish people. It has helped me know more and be more interested in my Christian background. I feel it's been good for me.

When I was growing up in the church and teaching Sunday school, one thing that always stood out in my mind in learning about Jesus Christ was that he was a Jew. At the time I didn't know what that meant, because I didn't know any Jewish people. Knowing the Jewish people, I think I've come to have a feeling of what kind of person Jesus Christ was. I'm not sure I'm explaining what I'm trying to say, but I have more of a feeling of the tradition, of the scriptures, of the relationships between the Old Testament and the New Testament.

APRIL 14, 1979

❋ 10 ❋

Mankind Is Improving

BERNARD FREUND

Bernard Freund earned a law degree from the University of Michigan in 1935, practiced law in California and Washington, and after World War II returned to Muncie to help operate his father's chain of clothing stores, which he liquidated in 1975. In the early 1970s he served as director of Muncie's Human Rights Commission. At the time of this interview in 1979 he was serving in the newly created position of "attorney for students" at Ball State University.

My maternal grandparents' parents settled in Muncie in the early 1880s. My grandmother's parents migrated with her to Indianapolis from Eastern Europe in the 1860s, when she was a baby. My grandfather migrated to Indianapolis later. He met my grandmother when she was about sixteen. They married, moved to Muncie and had five children here—three boys and two girls. One of the girls, Pearl, was my mother.

My mother's family lived here until the early part of this century, when the older two boys, who were in the scrap metal business with their father, left Muncie to open a successful iron and steel scrap brokerage in Chicago. They called for my grandfather to come join them, so he moved to Chicago with his family about 1908.

My paternal grandfather had been an officer in the German Army and was unhappy with military life, so to get way from the militaristic Prussian atmosphere he came to this country in 1894. He was an optometrist by trade who settled in Decatur, Illinois, with my grandmother, my Aunt Ella, and my father, who was then five years old.

My parents were married at age twenty-two and nineteen and lived in Chicago for several years. My father was a traveling salesman in the Chicago area for the Crown Overall Company of Cincinnati. During World War I, he didn't have much to do because of the shortage of denim needed by the armed forces, and after the war it was suggested to him that he move his family to Muncie, where my maternal grandparents owned a business block on the corner of Seymour and Walnut, where a successful clothing store had stood. At that time, in the '20s, that was the Bowery District—Muncie's "red light" district, where the gangsters for which Muncie was known tended to hide out. Dillinger was known to have frequented Muncie at the height of his career.

I recall on my tenth birthday my mother taking me on the train down from Chicago to live in Muncie—where my father had already moved—to open the store. And I've lived here the rest of my life, except for college, law school, and brief periods in Los Angeles and Washington and over three years' army service during World War II.

My father was a workaholic with a very high-strung temperament. He was constantly driving to make a success of himself, which would be the goal of most immigrants, particularly of Jewish background. The store was a work clothing store, for farmers and factory workers. His goal was to create a chain of successful clothing stores. By 1928 he had opened one or two additional stores in other towns. In 1939 he opened a store in Elwood for a cousin of ours, Martin Blumenthal, who was fleeing the Holocaust.

I can recall when I was in high school, getting up early to open the store. We opened at seven o'clock because factory workers would stop in to buy double-palmed Indianapolis gloves—at 19 cents a pair—that they would need for going to work, and I'd be there to sell them.

*

Neither my paternal nor maternal grandparents observed the Jewish laws, dietary or otherwise. We would have Jewish cooking appropriate to various festivals—Passover and Hanukah. But observing the—what is it, 631 or 613?—rules that Orthodox Jews worry about, that was never up for discussion in our family.

I attended Jewish Sunday School whenever there was one. Our congregation, then as now, was served by weekend rabbis or rabbinical students. Sometimes a circuit rider would serve several synagogues, other times a student from Hebrew Union College in Cincinnati would come here on weekends.

There were one or two years when we had no Sunday School, and in those years I can recall attending a Christian Science Sunday school. In my time there was a B'nai B'rith Youth Organization, and Aleph Zadik Aleph had a group which attracted Jewish youngsters from Muncie, Anderson, and Marion.

The social life of the Jews of that day was pretty centered. Of the sixty or seventy or eighty Jewish families who lived here, very few socialized with non-Jewish friends to any extent. So the question was which Jewish families you tended to be most friendly with. I recall that there was a very active Jewish social group. It included most of the merchants who owned stores on Walnut Street. My mother—who considered herself not quite in the top social group of the congregation—called them "The 398," as distinguished from "The 400."

In my youth, social relationships between Jews and non-Jews were pretty formal and pretty much non-existent. I was not active socially in high school. There were a few occasions when I wanted to go to a dance or some social event and there were only one or two Jewish girls my age to invite, and I didn't necessarily find them attractive. So from time to time I would ask non-Jewish girls to be my date, and most of the time I was turned down. And from the way I was refused, I got the distinct impression that it was because the girl either had acquired an anti-Jewish bias or knew that her parents would object.

I met my wife, the former Ruth Field of Fort Wayne, through a short-lived organization called the Indiana Union of Jewish Youth, which existed for the purpose of enabling young Jewish people from other cities to meet each other so they could possibly get married to each other, and that's the way it worked out for us.

*

In the '20s I wasn't of an age to know the extent of the Ku Klux Klan's influence. But I distinctly recall a Saturday night when I was working at my dad's store—at that time we stayed open until ten on Friday and Saturday—and a torchlight parade passed. White-robed Klansmen with hoods were marching along, and I stood there and looked at them, knowing that they represented hatred of Jews and Negroes and Catholics.

I can recall one incident in my early teens where I was on roller skates and a boy a little bit older than I chucked me down and called me a dirty Jew. That stuck in my mind. But it was the only incident that I can call overt anti-Semitism.

The restrictive covenants against Jews on real estate were not enacted by the government. They were placed in deeds by individuals or by developers, including Charles Bender, who was one of the most ardent enforcers of restrictive covenants.

*

The Green Hills Country Club started around 1950 basically because Jews were not accepted at the Delaware Country Club and we wanted an alternative. I would not myself have been happy with an exclusively Jewish country club, although I know there are many such around the country. But even if the others *had* preferred an all-Jewish country club, it wasn't feasible here because there weren't enough Jews to support a country club. So it was started as a community country club from the very beginning.

I was a member of the board for several years. I was treasurer of the construction company that saw to the planning and the physical work of creating greens and fairways. I made out the payroll checks during that period, and I was subsequently a member of the board.

I resigned from the board—although not from the country club—in about 1955, because the board refused to accept the membership of a black applicant. Actually, I think the decision was reached without an actual applicant. I think I just raised the issue. I said I knew of a black applicant who was perfectly acceptable. There weren't very many blacks in Muncie who could afford to join a country club, but I was friendly with several families, and I knew of one who I felt would like to join. I said to the board, "Now, if I invite him, will he be accepted?" And the issue was debated, and the answer was no.

Every one of those who voted "No" said, "Now, it isn't that I'm prejudiced, but the club is on very shaky financial ground"—which it continued to be until it went out of existence recently—"and if we accept blacks, we'll lose a good portion of our membership who are prejudiced." My attitude was: Well, that's tough—admitting blacks should take priority.

*

When I was growing up, my father was very much an assimilationist, not a Zionist. He believed in the great American dream. He was of limited education—he didn't finish high school—but he was so bound up in overcoming prejudice against Jews that for some years he paid for ads with the help of the Anti-Defamation League, and he would write articles and editorials on brotherhood and why it's wrong to hate people. If he had had the opportunity for higher education, I suspect he might have gone into some kind of social field.

I, on the other hand, am supportive of a homeland for the Jewish people. I don't see how anyone who has had any comprehension of the sad history of the Jewish people in the Western world can't be sympathetic to the need for some place the Jew can find a haven, and the only sure haven is a Jewish country.

*

I've been president of Temple Beth El congregation on two occasions, and I've been chairman of its community relations for probably fifteen years. For some time, when there was a lot of interest among churches in learning more about Judaism, I was kept very busy arranging visits. But that seems to have faded somewhat in recent years.

The congregation here is about half the size it was when I was young. There's quite a turnover in the population. Every year we have a number of families coming in, but every year we have a number of families moving out, and over the years there has tended to be a net deficit. I think now there are probably not more than forty or forty-five families listed as members of the congregation, whereas there were as many as ninety families at one time.

I can recall as a youngster in the '30s a very significant congregational meeting. Alex Shonfield, then in his eighties, was a member of a very well-known Jewish family. He stood before the congregation and made a point that still lingers in my mind: "The congregation is not growing larger; in fact it is growing smaller." That was over forty years ago, and I think it's accurate to say that as the years have gone by it *has* grown smaller.

*

For about fifteen years, I've been the liaison between the synagogue and the Jewish students on the Ball State campus. They call me the "lay religious advisor" to the Jewish students.

As far as I know, there have never been as many as a hundred Jewish students at Ball State.[1] There's a computer printout of the names of those who indicated a religious preference; there's never been more than seventy or seventy-five on that list.

Now, it's possible that half again as many, or twice as many, Jewish students are on campus who for one reason or another do not indicate their Jewish preference—sometimes because they don't want to be known as Jews, but more often, I think,

---

[1] On a campus of some 18,000 students, at the time of the interview (1979).

because they feel it's an unwarranted intrusion on their private life. I've had some Jewish students say they didn't put it on there because they thought that meant they would be assigned a Jewish roommate in the dorm, and they felt they were coming to college to broaden their experience with a non-Jewish group.

*

I don't have a lot of confidence in what the future will hold—either in Muncie, Indiana, or in small towns generally throughout the country. I think maybe Muncie has more of a holding action than other communities. I think perhaps Marion has gone downhill faster. There are practically no Jewish families left in New Castle; the population in Anderson keeps going down. I don't know what the situation is in Richmond. In the country as a whole, I have a feeling that the future of Judaism is by no means assured as a significant part of American life.

There's been a tremendous intermarriage rate during recent years. Of course, in many of those the non-Jewish member converts and becomes an active part of the Jewish community. But in many others, it works the other way.

Then, too, I have the observation that religion plays a smaller part in the life of Americans today than it did fifty years ago. I know there's been sort of a counter-movement—the great interest in personal faith in God and Jesus, and we see something like that in Asia in the re-emergence of fundamentalist Islam. But I guess it's just because of my own predilections, I can't believe it's going to continue—I don't think it makes sense in the real world to have such an unworldly approach to life. Since I tend to have a positive view of mankind, I believe that as time goes on, mankind is improving and life is getting better, and there's more kindness and more love.

MARCH 14, 1979

❊ 11 ❊

"There Was No Other Temple"

EDITH GARFIELD

Edith Garfield grew up in Muncie, the daughter of Sam Gold, a successful clothing merchant. She earned a law degree in 1938 from Indiana University, where she met her husband, a medical student. They subsequently moved to Indianapolis, where she administered her husband's medical office and where this interview was conducted. Both her daughters live in California.

My father was from Poland, my mother from Russia. They came to Indianapolis because some of their family was already here. My father went into the clothing business here with his brother. Apparently an opportunity in the junk business opened up in Muncie—that was a great opportunity at the time—and so they moved to Muncie and went into the junk business with another Jewish man—a Mr. Zeigler. After some years, my father went out of the junk business and opened a clothing store, which he ran in Muncie until his retirement.

His store catered to the working man, and I think it stood him in good stead to be in that type of business when the Depression came along, because even when times were bad, the working man always needed clothes, and my father had a moderately-priced store. It was a very plain store, and people felt comfortable about coming in. I know that some of the so-called "haberdashers," who were in more elegant surround-ings, closed down during the Depression. But my father got through all the bad times, and he was really quite successful in many ways.

He was a recognized businessman, a recognized member of the community, a recognized citizen. He served on the Hous-ing Board in Muncie and was very highly respected by every-one who knew him. He came to Muncie without any money and, on his own endeavor, he was able to buy real estate there. He owned quite a bit of real estate in Muncie, and I think he would have been considered one of the most successful busi-nessmen in the city.

In the beginning, my parents weren't active in Muncie's Jewish community because, with their Eastern European back-ground, they felt that they didn't really quite fit in with the Jewish community that was there then, which was more or less of a German extraction. The Germans were Reform Jews; my parents considered themselves Orthodox Jews. The Muncie Jewish community was perhaps just a little different from other communities in that the majority of Jewish people here were Reform.

The way I was brought up, Jewish values were quite im-portant —and I think that was the reason we didn't feel com-fortable in the Reform temple in the early years. The Reform Jews at that time—the German Jews—didn't place a value on the traditions of Judaism. There wasn't a representative group from the Orthodox branch, so in the early years I really had very few friends [in Muncie], except school friends, because there weren't any other Orthodox families there. And for the same reason, I didn't go to Sunday school. I didn't have too many friends because there were just no young people there. As I recall, there were only about three or four other young Jewish people my age.

But as time went on and there was no other temple for my parents to attend but the Reform temple, they did join, and they became much more active in the community. It wasn't that they compromised their own Judaism. I think Jews are Jews, and it's just a little different way of expressing the religion. My parents liked the more traditional approach, so on the High Holidays they came in to Indianapolis, where the service was more traditional. But for the weekly service, *bar mitzvahs,* and confirmations, they did attend temple in Muncie.

As I recall—you know, it's been a good many years—my mother did work at the temple. She'd help in the kitchen, and she'd sell tickets for various affairs. They were fairly active in the community.

Their close friends were practically all Jewish. They had many friends and acquaintances, but the people they saw on a regular basis were Jewish.

Most of my friends were non-Jews. They were the people I saw at school every day. Our evenings were really more family evenings, with my parents, my brother-in-law and sister [Archie and Ida Lapin], and my aunt and uncle, who lived in Muncie then. We spent more of our evenings with our family than we did with outsiders.

*

In reading *Middletown,* I've learned that there was a great deal of anti-Semitism in Muncie. But as I grew up, I never felt it at all. At school, I felt very well accepted by my acquaintances. Perhaps I wasn't looking for anti-Semitism, and that's why I didn't feel it. I never felt that I was excluded from anything because of my religion.

Of course, I don't remember ever being asked to join any of the clubs or sororities in high school. But I never really wanted to anyway. I didn't feel the need for that kind of organization, so I didn't feel excluded.

I can't say for certain that this was also true of my parents. My mother certainly never ran into any problems.

I understand there's been a great change in Muncie's Jewish community since I left. There are many more Jewish people there, but they're people I don't know—they're affiliated with the university.

*

I met my husband while I was in law school at Indiana University. He's from Atlantic City, New Jersey. He came to Indiana University because it was a little hard to get into medical school at that time, and he had an uncle living here in Indianapolis. You needed some address in Indiana in order to get in, so he came out here to live with his uncle and get his medical education that way.

Today my husband and I are affiliated with the Reform temple here in Indianapolis. So we've gone full-circle on that. But Reform Judaism has changed a great deal. The rituals you see in Reform temples today are not the kind of rituals that would have been accepted in the Reform temples of thirty or forty years ago. I think the Holocaust has changed a great deal [of things]. It's made us much more conscious of our identity, and we're not trying so hard to assimilate.

MAY 14, 1979

✳ 12 ✳

Reform vs. Orthodox

Pearl Shonfield

As the local treasurer of the National Foundation for Infantile Paralysis, Pearl Shonfield's late husband, Ray Shonfield, who died in 1972, was instrumental in distributing the first polio vaccine to Muncie schoolchildren in 1955. She was interviewed at her home in Indianapolis.

I was born and raised in Fort Wayne. I came from a very poor family. My father was in the upholstery and furniture business. There were nine children in our family and I had just two years of college. My brothers went for six and eight years, because they were doctors, and my family believed in the boys getting all the education. I taught school there. I first came to Indianapolis when I was sixteen to go to Madam Baker's School for Girls, which later affiliated with Butler University but is no longer in existence. Madam Baker was an old-time teacher who started the kindergartens in our state. We had chapel every morning, and we sang all the songs and she preached that there is no such thing as a bad child. When she died that year, I transferred to Ypsilanti State Normal College [now Michigan-Eastern College] for one year. I went with practically nothing to these two schools. My brothers and sisters helped me get two years of education. Then I taught for two years at Harrison Hill School in Fort Wayne before I got married.

*

My husband's grandparents, Rudolph and Rachel Shonfield, had a small dress factory many years ago in Muncie. Then his parents came in [to the business]. His father Lou and my husband went to the Jefferson School. After they were in Muncie a while, my father-in-law went into a men's clothing business with a brother-in-law in Columbus, Indiana, and lived there for a short time. That's where my husband, Ray Shonfield, was born. Shortly afterward they moved to Muncie, and Ray lived there until he went into the music business. Before he even graduated from high school, he went to Cuba with a group of high school kids called the Riley Orchestra. From there my husband went into bigger things in the music business.

I met Ray when I came to Indianapolis for a teachers' convention. He was playing the clarinet in a band called Charley Davis's Band. I was only seventeen and I saw him on the stage and said, "I want him for my husband." I didn't even know he was Jewish; I just fell deeply in love with him. I taught for two years and then he quit the music business. He was a very artistic man, and it was my family's fault that he gave up his artistic ability, because they frowned upon anyone who played in a band. He played in the Muncie Symphony for a while.

When we got married in 1930, he went back to Muncie and went into the Shonfield's Clothing Store downtown with his father. My father-in-law rented the store from Sam Gold—Edith Garfield's father. He was a very shrewd businessman who came from the old country and bought up most of Muncie. He was a very rich man and left his children lots of money. Those people who came from those other countries—Poland, Russia, and many of those others—were shrewder and smarter than these German-Jewish people, who were so-so wonderful that they looked down upon these [Eastern European] people. But they were not money-making people. I can remember my husband's aunts and all just never thought any of these [Eastern European] people who came

there were good enough for them to associate with. This is
ridiculous, but this is the way it was in Muncie.

My father-in-law was in the clothing business many years
before World War I and made what at that time was quite a bit
of money. He decided he was going to retire and sit on the
porch and rock. He sold his business to Sam Ringold, who also
made a lot of money there. Then when we got married, my
father-in-law helped my husband go into the men's clothing
business again and stayed in the store with him.

They carried the nicest merchandise, and my husband was
a highly respected citizen. When they wanted to do anything
downtown for the business district, it was my husband who
did it. He gave up his store to work for the polio organization [the March of Dimes] for years. Whenever people wanted
to know anything about polio they would come to my husband. We would go together to see these people in their iron
lungs. It was through Ray that these youngsters would have
teachers come out and help them, with just their heads stick-
ing out of their iron lungs—getting their education that way.
And Ray saw to it that all this was paid for through the Polio
Foundation. I mean, I was teaching then—people didn't even
want their children to *have* this vaccine. He was on the Mission Board, the Red Cross board, the Visiting Nurse Association board. Almost every day there was something in the
papers about him.

*

My in-laws were involved in the Jewish community. They
gave the Torahs and the two great big chairs that are standing
there in the temple. They gave money to help build the temple
and pay for the windows. Then people came in like the Golds
and another group of people. You were going to talk to Mrs.
Garfield—she called me today and wanted me to meet with
her. I said, "I couldn't meet with you because our viewpoints
would be different." They wouldn't belong to our temple. They
wanted it to be an Orthodox community. Whether it was Orthodox or Reform, who gave a damn what it was? That part is

so superficial. If you are religious and believe in being a good Jew, you're a good Jew.

There were different viewpoints when these new people came. There was a lot of friction that went on for a while. This dates back to maybe 1928, 1929. There was a family by the name of Dobrow or Dobrowitz, and these people did not want to come to a Reform temple. They wanted it to be Orthodox. They tried to get the temple to change, but they were never successful. This was a Reform temple built by Reform Jews, and they would never let it change.

I myself am an agnostic. I was one in Fort Wayne when I was growing up, although none of my family was that way. My children never went with any Jewish people. The first time my son had a date with a Jewish girl was when he went to Indiana University. The first time my daughter had a date with a Jewish boy was when she went to the University of Colorado. Now, that's pretty bad!

My husband and I were active in the temple. But the things that are important in Judaism—having Judaism in your home, lighting your candles on Friday night, knowing that there is a Passover, observing these things—we never had in the Shonfield family, which is too bad. I don't regret it, but my family in Fort Wayne and most of the people in Muncie probably thought it was terrible.

My daughter is very observant. She goes to temple—let me say that—and she goes with Jewish people. Her husband came from a very Orthodox Jewish family. I don't know how much Judaism she has in her home.

*

Before my time there was a Jewish Aid Society [in Muncie], which eventually became the sisterhood. We'd go down to the temple and put on big dinners for fifty, seventy-five people with our own hands. We had no one to help us. We washed the dishes, we made the food, we did everything down there in order to try to make that community successful. There weren't many people who could give a lot of money.

The temple has more money now because there are Jewish families like Martin Schwartz's family who came in and were successful. Bernard Freund went into his father's business. He graduated as a lawyer but never practiced law one day.[1] Bernard is a very brilliant man.

These people were very hard on our rabbis who came in. First we had a tri-city rabbi [for Muncie, Marion, and Anderson] called Rabbi Freund. Then we had a rabbi who married my children—I don't remember his name. Most of the very intelligent people made life miserable for these rabbis. I don't know why. This had nothing to do with the conflict between Orthodox and Reform. They probably felt they [the rabbis] just weren't smart enough for them, or they felt that the rabbis' wives ought to get in there too and work for the community. Some of the rabbis' wives couldn't do it, and there was a lot of friction and I didn't like it.

*

I loved teaching school, but I taught because I had to have more money to help my family have a beautiful home and to go with the kind of people they went with, who were at that time the so-called "best" people in Muncie, in Westwood. Very great, wonderful people.

I taught in Muncie at two [elementary] schools. I came to Indianapolis in 1963. At that time I was on a pretty high salary schedule, and it was hard to get work because they weren't hiring teachers. I taught at the Grandview School [in Indianapolis] for eight years. Then my husband became very sick and I quit.

*

We were supposed to buy a lot from a Mr. Doading in the Kenmore section of Muncie. The whole thing went through—was all signed and everything. The lot was bought and all the

---

[1] Bernard Freund actually practiced briefly in Los Angeles, Washington, and Muncie.

plans made with our builder and everything. But there was a
Charles Bender there at that time who would not let Jews into
Kenmore, and he took it off.

They would not let Jews at one time come into the Delaware Country Club. The Fort Wayne Country Club took Jews;
my family belonged there.

*

I belonged to a bridge club of twelve women [in Muncie];
I was the only Jewish woman. I hear regularly from my non-
Jewish friends from Muncie. I don't hear from any Jewish
people.

There was a reason. When I first came to Muncie there was
a different class of Jewish people there—the kind that I could
communicate with. After I was there a while, different people
came in with whom I could not communicate—people who
made a lot of money. Culturally, educationally, their viewpoints
about things—they were not the kind of people that I enjoyed
being with. I always looked down upon the moneyed [Jewish]
people, who are extremely wealthy people now in Muncie, who
I don't think would care whether anything was carried on in
the right way or not. They came from other communities. They
came from other big cities. Some of them came from the East,
and we Midwestern people always thought we were different. And we were. And a lot of them we didn't accept.

I was a teacher, so I went with a lot of the teachers there.
Today I go with a group of twelve teachers [in Indianapolis]
who meet every Monday, and I'm the only Jewish one. They
are people who give a lot of travelogue talks here, who are
very educated, who are much younger than I. I'm seventy years
old; these other people are all in their forties and fifties, but I
still belong with them, and I enjoy their company.

MAY 14, 1979

❖ 13 ❖

An Instinct for Survival

Burle Plank

Burle Plank came to the Muncie area from Russia as a four-teen-year-old in 1922. His boyhood resourcefulness at surviving in Russia during the famines following the Revolution was subsequently put to good use as he built a scrap iron business as well as several other businesses in Muncie. He was a long-time leader of Muncie's Jewish community and an active participant in Muncie civic affairs.

My father came to this country in 1912. His in-laws—my mother's sister and her husband—had emigrated from Russia to Bluffton, Indiana.[1] My uncle was in the scrap business in Bluffton, and he put my father in the same kind of business. He bought him a horse and wagon and he went out to get scrap. When my father came to this country he left my mother and five children [including me] behind in Russia. He didn't have very much money, and to become a citizen of this country you had to be here five years. So it was difficult for him to

---

[1] A county seat town of 8,000, about forty miles north of Muncie.

do very much the first five years. Then World War I broke out, making it impossible for him to bring his family to this country [until the war was over]. And after the war it was very difficult to get out of Russia because of the revolution.

My father migrated from Bluffton to Pennville, Indiana.[2] He had a place of his own there, and then he finally came to Montpelier,[3] where he settled with a business and got acquainted with a banker in Hartford City,[4] where he was doing business on a commission basis. This banker, Senator Watson, was friendly with Everett Watkins, the Washington correspondent for the *Indianapolis Star*. He also knew a man named Eli Strauss in Indianapolis who had a big clothing store, and later on Mr. Schloss became the Morris Plan of Indianapolis. He was interested in working with Mr. Watkins and Senator Watson, and I think they helped my dad finally get his second [citizenship] papers [in 1921]. Through their efforts we were able to come to this country in 1922. If a husband became a naturalized American citizen, then his wife and his children automatically became American citizens. That law was changed in '22 [after we arrived].

When I came to this country I was fourteen years old and had gone through the Russian Revolution and the starvation, and I had no formal education. I did have some Jewish tutoring when I was six years old. But right before the revolution we moved out of our village, Bavivnitz—I don't know how you spell it—to live quite a distance from there with our mother's brother in Astrakhan on the Volga River. At the time of the Revolution I was about nine years old. My mother and I used to get up at two or three o'clock in the morning and buy fish. And we would carry the fish maybe two miles and spread out the fish on burlap bags in the morning and sell fish.

---

[2] A village of 700 about twenty-five miles northeast of Muncie.
[3] A town of about 2,000, about twenty-five miles north of Muncie.
[4] A county seat town of 8,000, seven miles south of Montpelier and about twenty miles north of Muncie.

I had an education in survival in Astrakhan. After the Revolution it was almost impossible to get bread or flour, because everything was burned and destruction was every place. A lot of cannibalism was going on—people eating humans—it's almost hard to describe. But I found out that farmers had food. They had flour and wheat to sell, but there was no way to get it to the market. And they had no clothes. No one was allowed to move or leave town unless you had emergency visas. I don't know how I got this information, but I took some clothes, like shirts and dresses and things like that, and I made a little bundle and hopped on a train with the soldiers.

At my age I was small in stature, so on the first trip I crawled in the oil box underneath the train for probably 150 miles. When I felt I was far enough from Astrakhan, I got out. Everybody is good to a boy or a girl, so the soldiers would feed me. I took my bundle and I got into the country, and I traded my clothes to the farmers for flour. I probably carried thirty or forty pounds. Then I worked my way back to Astrakhan on another train going the other way.

I'd say I did that about a year and a half. I know one time my uncle saw an announcement in the paper that they caught and executed two people at the station and needed to identify them. And here I was on a trip. You can imagine what went on. My mother and my uncle went down to the railroad station and checked the corpses to see if they could find me. And the next day, here I come. And I wouldn't let my mother let me in the house because I was full of lice. I undressed outside the house and had her burn my clothes. They were just absolutely covered with lice, and I brushed myself off before I went into the house.

To get food, my two sisters and my brother and I started to make cigarettes, which was illegal. In Russia you didn't buy them in a pack; they would come 200 cigarettes in a box. I used to peddle them. Then we found out where we could get the packaged cigarettes. I got arrested one day when I was about eleven, and they took me to the police station and pulled out my shirt and sent for my mother. They threatened to shoot me unless I told where I got those cigarettes. Well, if I would have told them, they probably would have killed those people. So I never did tell them. I was only eleven—what were they going to do with me?

The next day I was back out on the street, selling cigarettes. It was a matter of survival.

By this time the cigarette business was running down. Everything had its periods. One day when our cigarettes were not selling so good, I was out at the bazaar in the marketplace. There was another world there: people buying and selling, and the Russians peddling zucchini from the farmers, woolen socks and sweaters—they had everything, and people were buying, because most of the stores were burned out. It was real exciting to me to see how much business there was.

The next day I told my mother, "We're going to the bazaar at the market tomorrow, and I want you to go with me. We're going to sell cigarettes there." So she went with me. I took a burlap bag, just like the other merchants. You just spread a bag out on the street and put your stuff down, and you had a stand. I told my mother to stay there, and I took full boxes of cigarettes and started mixing with the people. I stopped a Russian *kulak* and asked him what he wanted for his woolen stockings. In the Russian system they would bargain back and forth and then slap hands. So I bought those wool stockings from him, and I was all excited—that's the first time I had ever done that. I started back to my mother to put the stockings on the burlap for a higher price. But before I got there somebody stopped me and wanted to know if the stockings were for sale. I gave them a price and they bought it, and I made a profit on it.

You can imagine how excited I was. I went over and told my mother how much money I had made just by buying and selling these woolen stockings. She could hardly believe it. That was my beginning; from then on we did quite well and were able to make a living.

Then I found out there was a shortage of bluing, that you wash clothes with. It came from Sirocca, about 300 or 400 miles from Astrakhan. You couldn't get any papers to go there, but I also found out that in Sirocca there was a shortage of herring and salt. Now, Astrakhan was the capital for salt mines; that's where they used to make caviar on the Volga, and having all the salt meant they could process the fish and ship it all over the world. So I found out that if I could get herring over to Sirocca I could sell the herring and buy bluing and get it back to Astrakhan.

I devised a plan that I would either go by train or by boat. I would buy two bags of herring, each weighing maybe 200 pounds per bag. I had the bags delivered to the dock and loaded on the ship. Then how was I going to get on? I had no ticket, no pass or anything.

I managed to get those two bags of herring on ship. Then there was a family going through with four or five kids. I went through with them, because I was so small that I was just another kid. In Sirocca I sold the herring on the dock and I found out where to get bluing, and then I worked my way back to Astrakhan by train.

When I brought this bluing home I was a big operator—nobody else had bluing. So I rationed out the bluing to some merchants in the market and I put a price on it: They had to sell it for so much a spoon. If they sold it for any less, I wouldn't sell them any more bluing. I made maybe half a dozen trips to Sirocca and I got by OK.

*

Then we got the final papers that we were going to go to the United States. So there I was, an American citizen living in Russia. When we came to the United States we did not go through all the rules that an immigrant has to, because we were American citizens.

From the boat [in New York] they transferred us to the New York Central station, and when we got there, here comes a man telling us that he was Mr. Everett Watkins, and he helped my dad bring us over. Well, we could not understand, we couldn't speak a word of English. So he got some interpreter from a Jewish agency in New York, and he was telling us who Mr. Watkins was, and of course we were so scared. They told us if we talked too much about Russia we would probably not be let into the United States, so we were scared to say anything.

Well, we finally opened up a little. Mr. Watkins gave us each a dollar, and he couldn't do enough for us. That man was wonderful. Leaving New York, we had to go by way of Columbus, Ohio, to come into Hartford City, and every place the train would stop, people would come and give us a present. See, Mr. Watkins was writing a story about the family that escaped from Russia and starvation and all of that.

In Columbus, Ohio, a Jewish family wanted to take us to their home. And of course we wouldn't move, we wouldn't let them get their hands on us—we didn't know who they were. They were so nice to us—they retained a young man to go with us on the train clear to Hartford City. It really wasn't necessary—we had tags on us. We got into Hartford City about three or four o'clock in the morning, and when we arrived this young man was gone. I guess he must have seen us fall asleep and he got off some place. But we really didn't need him.

When we got to Hartford City, the agent at the station didn't know what to do with us. He couldn't talk to us; we couldn't talk to him. Our ticket said our Russian name was "Plavonick" and he didn't quite interpret that. He put us in the station, and it finally dawned on him that he remembered reading that Max Plank's family was coming. So he called my dad, and of course he came over and took us home to Montpelier.

I was fourteen years old; I had an older brother who was eighteen, a sister who was sixteen and another sister who was twelve (we lost a little girl in Russia about six months after I left). But I was the leader. Why, I don't know; it just happened like that.

We enrolled in the Huntington School in Montpelier—all but my oldest brother: He wouldn't go because he felt ashamed to go in with the kids. At the first enrollment, I was in first grade, believe it or not, with the tots. The next day they moved me into the second grade, and before the season was over I went through all the grades. The following year I went through all but high school—that would be the eighth grade. I had real good grades in math, and I was very fortunate that I had good teachers who had patience and helped me and kept me after school. They would show me a picture—a table, a chair, with the word spelled beneath it, and it would all tie in. Everybody was wonderful. It was a small community, and having a strange family like ours—it would probably never happen again like this in the whole country in my whole life.

*

When I finished the eighth grade, my dad and my brother and I decided we would open up another scrap yard in Hartford City. I was going along to high school, but my brother and dad got in an argument—you know how young boys are—and he just took off and left us. So at sixteen years old I was stuck with the business in Hartford City and I couldn't go back to school.

Well, you know, when you're young you see girls, and they're attractive. I found a girl from a nice Quaker family. They lived on a farm, and I used to go out there quite a bit. Mrs. Kelsey was a graduate of Vernon College in 1900, and not many people graduated college in those days. They had three daughters and three sons, and I had been going to school with one daughter and one son. So when I told them I couldn't go back to school, Mrs. Kelsey actually cried that my father was doing me an injustice by sacrificing an education that I probably would never get. So I made a promise. I said, "Now, Mrs. Kelsey, I will get an education some way."

"Well," she said, "it doesn't usually work out like that."

Well, her daughter (not the girl I was interested in) was on a trip. She was an English teacher for DuPont's[5] private school

---

[5] E. I. DuPont & Co., the major chemical concern based in Wilmington, Delaware.

in Wilmington, Delaware, and every year she would take a bunch of people to Europe as a tour guide. But then she took a leave of absence for a year because she wasn't feeling too good, so Mrs. Kelsey insisted that her daughter teach me while she was home.

So that's what happened: After I got home from Hartford City each day, I'd clean up, get something to eat and drive out in the country about five miles, in a Model T Ford, to a mile east of Keystone. I'll tell you, many times I went out there I didn't know if I was going to make it, the snow was so bad. But I made it; I was determined to get an education.

We were in Hartford City five years. Then my brother and I opened up a business in Muncie in 1929. By this time I had developed reading habits. I would always read a lot of things. When I got to Muncie I wanted to further my education, so I looked up the Emerson private school here. I got ahold of Mrs. Emerson and worked out a deal with her where she would teach me at home. I used to go there twice a week, then once a week. After two years she said, "I can't teach you any more," and she kicked me out.

All this time I was working, too. But I had made a promise to Mrs. Kelsey, and I kept my promise. She finally passed away about two years ago; she was ninety-six or ninety-seven. From the time I met this woman until she died, every year I'd send her a bouquet of poinsettias at Christmas. At the end she was in a nursing home in Richmond [Ind.] for a couple of years, and it just broke my heart to see her pretty well crippled up and in a wheelchair. I told her I always considered her as my second mother, and she cried and said, "I was always proud of you."

*

There were two other Jews in Montpelier; both had men's clothing stores. One sold dress clothing and the other had work clothing. They lived there and they stayed there; they were well respected in the community; and if they wanted to go to religious services, they used to drive to Marion or Fort Wayne (where my parents went) or Indianapolis.

My mother and father were strictly Orthodox. My father never worked a Saturday all his life that he lived in this country. He would close his business Friday night and would never open it until Monday morning. And my mother kept kosher. She would get her meats from Fort Wayne, and later when they moved to Muncie she would get them from Indianapolis. They would not eat meat in a restaurant; they would probably order cheese or eggs, something like that. And I'd say I and the rest of the family, except for my oldest sister, followed the pattern of my parents. My sister lived in Muncie, and her husband worked for us for over forty years. They too observed the kosher tradition, but outside they would eat non-kosher meat. But at home it was always kosher.

I took the position that to be honest with myself I could not eat kosher. Because I'm involved in business, I have to go out and eat with business people, and it's hard to stick to a kosher diet or adhere to the Sabbath on Saturday. I felt that if I couldn't follow all the rules, that wouldn't mean I wasn't a good Jew. I felt I was doing my part in another way. And I felt that Reform Judaism and its way of life fitted into my picture, and I was fortunate that my wife felt the same way (although her parents also were strictly Orthodox). So we never kept kosher; we did everything everybody else did. We'd even drive on Saturday. It would be impossible for me to live out here if I couldn't drive a car.

I find, and my wife finds, that Reform Judaism fits into our way of life. We feel very strongly about Reform Judaism. I think the future of Judaism in this country is following the pattern set by Reform movements. Maybe Israel is going to turn that around, but basically I think the Jewish leaders in this country come from Reform Judaism.

*

In Muncie my brother and I were, I would say, successful, and I branched out into a lot of businesses. I was in the finance business, the manufacturing business, the furniture business, and the automobile business. I got rid of some here not too many years ago. You know, smart as you might think you are, you make mistakes, too. But while I was doing all that, I didn't forget the fortunate thing that I am an American and I live in a great country, and the country gave me the opportunity, and I gave of myself wherever I could. I served our [Temple Beth El] congregation. Harry Zeigler and I organized the Jewish Welfare Fund, and I was chairman about four or five times and treasurer for about twenty-five years. Then I was president of the B'nai B'rith, and I was president of our temple for eighteen years. I was also chairman of the Muncie Red Cross, and I worked on the United Fund many times, and also on a drive for Ball State [Teachers College, now Ball State University]. That was when they were putting up the [Emens] Auditorium [c. 1964]. I gave money like everybody else did. But it's not what you can give yourself, so much; it's how you can get other people to give.

*

The other thing I did—the Delaware Country Club would not accept Jews as members. I felt there should be a place a Jewish person could belong if he wanted to play golf. My wife's cousin was married to Morton Standt, a golfer. He was more interested in golf than I was. We were talking one day, and an opportunity presented itself: Green Hills Farms, which Arthur Ball owned at one time—about 800 acres—was up for sale. I got the call from a real estate man, and I picked up Morton Standt and Ben Hertz, who owns Midwest Towel. We drove out to Green Hills Farms, and before we left that afternoon we bought 147 acres of the lodge and home and the grounds. We built that country club, and I would say I spent about six months the first year, building and supervising, buying, raising funds—we were almost living out there. I could say that I personally raised 50 percent of the money that went into that club. And I enjoyed doing it.

It wasn't a Jewish country club because we don't have enough Jews. This was done so the community could have another country club. I got the money from non-Jews as well as Jews—people like the bank presidents and all the industry people. They didn't turn me down. I was the first president of Green Hills, and I was treasurer for twenty years, and I felt that was enough. Unfortunately, Green Hills was just sold. And it just about broke my heart. It was a million-dollar plant sold for $300,000. It's a beautiful place. Something was wrong. They couldn't run it. No leadership.

*

When I was president of Beth El Temple I used to tutor religion for ten or eleven years. I invited all the ministers from the county and surrounding counties to our temple, and I would bring in an outstanding speaker—a professor from Hebrew Union College [in Cincinnati] or some outstanding rabbi. We'd have a seminar where the ministers had a chance to ask questions. I used to spend the whole day with them. We'd start at ten, then the sisterhood would have a luncheon, and then there'd be a program from one to four. I was doing that basically to break down prejudice. This community was once a hotbed for the Ku Klux Klan. So I felt that if we can open the door and let people see that Jews are human beings who want the same things that everybody else wants, then we can learn from each other and really live better together. And I think it's worth it. Now Delaware Country Club takes in Jews, the Muncie Club takes in Jews, now Jews can buy a home or land in Westwood or Kenmore. So I think all the things that were done helped cement relationships between Jews and non-Jews.

But of all the Jews in the community, there were only a few who would cooperate and help in any program that would benefit the community. You couldn't get everybody to even think the same way that you're thinking. But basically I think that's the way everything works in this country. It takes a few people to start a ball rolling.

*

Years ago the [Jewish] social life was much better than it is now. The old group would get together and socialize with cards, dinners, or dances. But now we have a little different group of people here. Like Mort Pazol said, at one time you could walk down Walnut Street and meet all the Jews. Well, that has changed. Most of those merchants are gone. Very few of their children have stayed here; they've migrated to bigger cities. So today we have faculty from Ball State, we have some manufacturers, we have a few people here and there. Not to discredit the Jews before, but I think we have a higher educated group than we had then.

We moved my dad and mother to Muncie [from Montpelier] in 1935, when they were getting up in years. My father was a nice man, but he didn't have a formal education. In his own way he was a scholar as far as the Jewish faith. But we're getting a different class [of Jews] now. They're more modernized. Let's say more Americanized.

*

My relationship with the non-Jews in the community has been very good. I've had [gentile] business associates, and I was involved in several community projects. I never felt any anti-Semitism or embarrassment because of my religion. Anti-Semitism in Muncie was something that developed probably prior to my coming here. There must be some reason for that, and I never did find out why those discriminatory things were in effect. Maybe some Jewish person did something wrong, and you establish a hatred. Of course, Jews have been persecuted for centuries, maybe for no reason at all.

*

I think [my wife and I] are good Jews as far as Judaism goes. We work for the Jewish cause, and we also work for the community cause. Wherever we are, we feel that we're Americans and we have to pay taxes like everybody else, and this is a great country, and anything that's necessary to do, we do it. And religion is something else.

At one time I was a Zionist for a year or two. My wife's family belonged to the Zionist Lodge. But as far as I'm concerned, the issue had never interfered with my life either way. The Zionist movement believes in Israel, and I do too. But I don't have to be a Zionist to be a Jew. I feel just like an Irishman. He comes from Ireland; he doesn't want to live there, but he wants to see Ireland survive as a country. In other words, you need some roots some place.

*

As long as there will be a Muncie there will be a Jewish community. Muncie has something to offer as a community. It's a good business town, and we have a lot of industry here, and there's no reason why a Jew couldn't come here and be part of the community and make a living here. I feel that wherever you live, if you are part of a community, then you are a happier person, because your community is your home.

We'll be married forty years next month, and we do not have children. Maybe if I had children I might think differently. But we certainly enjoy Muncie. I feel that this is my home, my community, and if there is anything I am able to do for Muncie, I'd try.

Sure, we have some families whose sons and daughters have moved away. But we've got new ones, and we've got some of the old ones who have stayed on, and there's no reason why they should have.

I have no heirs to take over my business. I have a nephew— my brother's son—but he has no interest; he's a musician in San Francisco. I've tried many times to get him to come down, but I haven't been successful. But he has two sons! It may be far-fetched, but I'm hopeful that one of his two sons might want to come in here some day and take a look. But if not, I look at it from another point of view: I only live for today. I do the best I can. I'm building a business. When my time comes and I have to leave this world, somebody will buy it. Whether he be a relative or a friend or a stranger, if it's successful it will go on, and if it's not—well, there's always going to be somebody to buy junk cars, whether Burle Plank is here or not.

FEBRUARY 22, 1979

✻14✻
A Jew Who Went Fishing

ALLEN BURGAUER

Allen Burgauer, second-generation partner in an office machines dealership started by his father in 1907, was born in Muncie in 1913.

My grandfathers were both from Germany and my grandmothers were both from Switzerland. My mothers' family settled in Vanessa, Pennsylvania, and my father's in Cleveland. I never met my mother's family, but after my father came to Muncie his family came to live here.

My parents met through a mutual acquaintance and were married when he was thirty-two and she was thirty. My father had been married once before, but not for very long. My father worked for an office machine dealer in Cleveland. He decided he would go out for himself. He'd come down in Indiana and would call on county seats and places probably once a year and ride to the end of the interurban. He never did drive a car; he owned some, but he never drove one. And that's how he happened to settle in Muncie later. He just thought it would be a good place to start.

He had a bad time, though. He actually had a place in Cleveland and a place here. And in those days a [business] place could actually be very small: half as big as this room, with practically no inventory. At that time the office machine business was a buying business. Even after I was grown some, it would gross about $5,000 or $6,000 business a year. Of course, he told me at that time that a man making $2 a day could raise a family and own his own home. But he didn't own a home until many years later, and that was a peculiar thing. When my mother's parents passed away, she had enough money in their estate to buy a house, and that's how they got the house— $4,000 for an eight-room house.

My dad was in the office machines business from 1907 to 1930, and I had worked other places before I went in there to work. When I was younger I worked in the fruit market, the clothing store, in a shoe store.

*

My wife, Bertha, is from Louisville, Kentucky. I met her right here in Muncie in 1938, when she was visiting her sister. That was a few days before Valentine's Day, and we got married May first.

I have to be real frank about it: If my wife hadn't come here visiting her sister, I might not have married Jewish. I wasn't interested in anybody, but by the same token there weren't any eligible Jewish girls here my age or anywhere near, and I just don't believe I could have gone to Indianapolis or Louisville or Chicago or any place to meet one.

*

Jewish life in Muncie then was a great deal different than in the city. Most of my friends, even as a kid, were non-Jewish, because where we lived they were all very friendly. But when I was a youngster, if people would get mad at you, they'd call you a dirty Jew. I never got in any fights over it, but I think it's different now. I know it's different.

I'll give you a little sample of why. When our daughter was born and my wife, Bertha, wheeled the baby up and down the sidewalk on the block, she'd meet a non-Jewish person about two doors from us. They'd talk a little bit, and then one day the woman said to my wife, "Bertha, I always thought Jewish people were different, but you're not different."

Most people wouldn't have known I was Jewish, except when something would come up and they'd ask me what church I go to. Then I told them I go to Jewish temple. And a lot of times I'd call on people and they'd say something about the Jews, and I'd always let them know I was Jewish, and they'd say, "Well, we didn't mean *you*."

When I was fifteen, sixteen years old I used to go down on Saturday evenings to a sporting goods store in town, run by a man named Earl Retz. When anybody new would come in there he hadn't introduced me to, he'd say, "Say, I want you to meet Allen Burgauer." Then he'd say, "Did you ever hear of a Jew that went fishing and hunting?" They didn't associate Jews with outdoor activities. All they associated them with was, "Probably they run some little business or something like that."

I don't fish as much as I did then. I did go fishing last summer some, and when I couldn't find anybody to go with me I went out anyhow and came home with a nice mess of fish.

*

Most of the Jewish people in a small community then, more so than even now, were peddlers and one thing or another who came here and opened some kind of little business. It's some kind of a misconception that Jewish people always had business—they didn't. In the bigger cities they worked just like anybody else for somebody else. But I didn't know that until I was older, when I went there [to cities] and saw [Jewish] people who worked for somebody else at a factory, in a tailor shop, in a department store.

Most of the Jews in Muncie were relatively successfully economically. But I also think that many other people, Jewish or otherwise, wouldn't have succeeded, because they wouldn't have done the things the [Jews] did then to succeed—for example, by having a store up-front and living behind the store, such as this.

I've got a friend around the corner, he keeps telling me that Jewish people are smarter than other people, but I couldn't say that. Well, maybe because they're a minority they just work harder at it.

*

My dad didn't belong to any clubs. The only club we've been in was the B'nai B'rith. He wasn't a real active Jew, and I'm not overly active. I don't belong to B'nai B'rith now because I never went to the meetings. I didn't see any reason to; I've always paid my dues, but I never went.

I don't think I would ever have gone to Sabbath school except for my mother. My dad just wasn't—he wasn't against anything; he just wasn't active at it.

I've always belonged to the temple. My mother always went to temple. But my father never went often. He was a believer in personal things; he was an upright, forthright man. He was a conservative like I am, only to a bigger degree.

*

I got interested in civic affairs by going to a Christian camp. When I was in high school, maybe a freshman or sophomore, I signed up for what was called "Bible study." I didn't know what it was, but it had a lot to do with Christianity. I guess we didn't believe in it, but I took a test and won a free week to Camp Crosley, the YMCA camp. Bernard Freund did, too; we both got 100 on the test. Later I went to the camp for another two weeks, and I got interested and joined the [Muncie] YMCA before my dad even knew I belonged. And later I got interested in the Camp Crosley alumni, and I'm still active in it. It's an organization that tries to use a little of your time and a little of your money to send boys to camp who can't afford to go.

*

In the future I think we'll find that mixed marriages are going to change the Jewish community. Quite often when you have a thing like that, you end up with neither of them going any place. I've got three sons, and none of the three have married Jewish. The oldest belongs to B'nai B'rith, and one of his daughters goes to temple. I think the Jewish community's going to get smaller and smaller, although there's a number of Jewish people that come to town that didn't originate here, including some at Ball State.

MARCH 20, 1979

❋ 15 ❋

Tending to Business

ROBERT BURGAUER

Robert Burgauer's father arrived in Muncie in 1907. He and his brother Allen represented the second of three generations operating Muncie Typewriter Exchange, later Burgauer's Office Equipment.

My dad was born in Cleveland, Ohio, and my mother came from Vanessa, Pennsylvania. He came in 1907 and set up a business. I think he originally financed it himself, but he may have had a little help from my mother. She was left some money from somebody through her estate, and she helped finance and operate the business.

I'd say the business was very successful. Nothing real big. It became much larger when my brother and I got involved. From the early twentieth century there's been a tremendous amount of changes. New types of equipment have come out and new lines were taken on. This is a real sophisticated period for electronic equipment. The typewriter was the foundation of my father's business, but it isn't the foundation of my business. When IBM got real strong in the typewriter business—electrics—to make any money of consequence in the typewriter business you were really forced to spread out into the cash register business to make it worthwhile.

*

There was not much social life in the Jewish community. I was never active in it. My mother participated in it as much as she could, but my father never was active. He didn't even go to temple. I'll put it to you this way. It was a struggle for my mother to be a member of the temple, because my father never wanted to pay the temple dues. He didn't think it was necessary.

But I received a Jewish education here at the Beth El Temple. I was confirmed. But the temple has not been real important to me. Most of my friends are non-Jewish.

*

In the days of my youth there were very few Jewish people here. Of the ones who were here, I would say most were in business for themselves as retail merchants. In my generation most of the Jews got an education beyond high school, but that wasn't so in my father's generation. But on my mother's side they did have a real education. She had two brothers who were doctors, and I think she had one brother who was a dentist.

*

I personally think the social life in the Muncie Jewish community has changed a tremendous amount over the last ten-twenty years. They used to have more things going on—card games and gatherings at the temple or in someone's home. You used to have a New Year's Eve party—all the Jewish people would go to the New Year's Eve party. I think it's just that a lot of the people have moved on to other cities, and they've died off, too. There was a time here when Muncie had a fairly decent-size Jewish population—nothing tremendous, but I'd say offhand there were eighty or ninety Jewish families at one time. Now you say there are fifty or sixty, but they must be hibernating someplace.

*

I met my wife in February 1940, at the Jewish Center in Indianapolis. Most of my Jewish activities were in Indianapolis, because there was not a nice Jewish girl here in Muncie. In those years I don't think there were more than two or three Jewish girls here in Muncie. I don't know if other young Jewish men went there for that reason. I was only interested in myself.

We were married in August 1941. I spent a year in the service, from 1943 to 1944, but I was discharged after being injured on maneuvers. I came back to Muncie and we had two children: Elaine, who is married, and my son Steve. Elaine is a housewife with three children, and my son's in business with me.

My wife came from an Orthodox home, but we didn't raise our children in an Orthodox home. The Jewish upbringing we gave our children rubbed off on me from being around her parents—to see how they lived, and how the family got along, and how close they were following the Jewish religion.

*

As far as I'm personally concerned, my relationship with non-Jews has not been bad at all over the years. I know there's been certain restrictions as far as Jewish people in Muncie are concerned—the Elks Club, the Delaware Country Club, and some others. I never was asked to join, so I was never turned down. But as far as having any problems with non-Jewish people in Muncie, I can't pinpoint anything in particular.

The only thing I remember is that years ago when we were getting ready to build a house in Kenmore, I was told, "There is no way you can build a house in Kenmore. They won't sell you the ground."

It so happened I had known the real estate man for many years. I went to him personally and told him I'd like to buy this lot that this house is on now. We went over to his home; we sat down and talked. My wife was with me. And he says, "Bob, you can buy anything I've got out here that you want."

I said, "Well, Charley, I was told that it would be 'sold,' because two other Jewish people in Muncie tried to buy out in this area. I just wanted you to tell me with your own mouth whether you'd sell to me or not."

He said, "Absolutely." He got up from his desk and went by the window. "Come over here, Bob," he said. "All this is out here; take your choice. Which one do you want?" I bought the lot in '53 and built in '54.

So in my lifetime I have never been involved in anything [anti-Semitic]. We've heard of two other cases where people were having some difficulty. But the fact is, we were told directly by somebody that they tried to buy some land down here, and they didn't believe we were going to get it, and we did get it. And it was no struggle—none at all.

The man who sold us this ground, may he rest in peace, I told him about this, and he was—let's put it this way: Most of the people in the Jewish community thought he was against the Jewish people. They really did, and I have no reason to think that he was or he wasn't. But the evidence is there: He wanted to sell me the ground, and with no strings attached. I had known this man for years. Don't forget, there were very few people here in town who were born and raised in Muncie.

*

I have not been that close to the Jewish community. I don't have the same interests. I like to go out and play golf. I go out with customers. I'm not a college graduate; I don't like to go to book reviews and discuss world history and all that. My years have all been spent with working, not with reading and getting all this knowledge. Perhaps I should have. But I'm doing exactly what I like to do.

The reason we love Muncie is, you like the place where you do well. If two people are married, and they're happy, and they're happy with their children, and their children are happy—you can pick your friends, but you can't pick your relatives.

APRIL 25, 1979

❋16❋

From Metropolis to County Seat

JOE FREADLIN

Joe Freadlin ran a store in Winchester, Indiana, twenty miles east of Muncie, which was opened by his father-in-law about 1923.

Both my parents, from the stories I recollect and remember being told, immigrated when they were very young, my father from Russia at the age of fifteen, my mother from Austria at the age of twelve. After passing through Ellis Island, they both ended up in the Bronx, where they had families. As was customary during that period, they immediately obtained employment to earn money for passage for the balance of their families. In their teens they met, fell in love, and were married and raised a family. I, one of three children, was born in the Bronx.

My father's occupation was tailoring for Hickey-Freeman Company in Rochester, New York, until World War II broke out. Then he went in as a civilian employee with the Navy, and he lived in Pensacola, Florida, where he worked for ten years until his retirement. Then because of health he moved to Atlanta with my sister. Now he is in a home for the Jewish aged in Atlanta with my mother.

My mother worked in the garment industry until she was married. Once they were married and raised the children, my mother never went back to work. It was the customary thing.

To the best of my knowledge, they never had any adjustment problems in Rochester. Rochester had a pretty large Jewish community, and they fitted in very easily. I think it was a clothing center at that time, particularly men's clothing, and jobs were easily available. My friends and my schoolmates there were primarily Jewish boys and girls.

Although we were of very strong Judaic background, we were not Orthodox or religious. We belonged to the Conservative branch. My grandparents were very religious; they had a kosher home. My parents did not. But we observed all the holidays. We went to the synagogue, not the temple, but we were not wholly religious.

We were not poor, but we were certainly not well off. As a boy in Rochester I had a number of jobs. I recall a paper route all through high school, and I worked at various soda fountains. The work ethic was extremely important in my family; so was education. In addition to being *bar-mitzvah,* I was sent to a *yiddishe* school to learn Jewish reading and writing. My sister was a cashier in a theater all through high school. She became a graduate nurse, and my younger sister worked so she could go to a college for secretarial work. It was stressed that we get as much education as we could possibly get on the basis of what we could afford.

I was interested in economic education, and a couple of my buddies and I applied to various schools. I was accepted at Syracuse; I was going to go there because an aunt lived there. But I and my other two buddies decided that since we had never been farther than a hundred miles from Rochester, we were all going to go west. Two of us ended up in

Illinois and one in Wisconsin. And we liked our schools and just stayed on.

I went to the University of Illinois and met my wife there. She was born in Elwood, Indiana, and her mother and father moved to Winchester when she was five for the purpose of starting their own business, which he did approximately in 1923. So she's practically a native of Winchester— she went through kindergarten, primary and high school and then afterward the university. My wife received her Jewish education, Sunday school and her confirmation at the Muncie Temple Beth El. Our daughter was one of the first Jewish girls born in Winchester, and her brother was one of the first Jewish boys.

When I first came to Winchester, the other Jewish families here were not my contemporaries; they were my parents-in-law's contemporaries. I remember meeting them socially and on the street, but there were no other Jewish people of our age, other than my wife's younger brothers.

The Jews I knew here [in Winchester] were in the clothing business also. They had a store in town. My father-in-law, my brother-in-law, and I have always been active in all the social groups, such as Rotary or Kiwanis. I've been a member of Rotary now for thirty-some years. We belong to the Masons, the Elks, the Scottish Rite, the whole rigmarole. And I was appointed to the school board for a four-year period.

When I first came here as a young man I asked my father-in-law about the relationship between the Jews and non-Jews, being a young Jewish boy from a large Jewish community coming to a community that was actually negligible as far as Jewish people were concerned. There really weren't any problems or any strong relationship being a Jew or a non-Jew, because there weren't too many Jews. There simply weren't very many. There was no particular problem, as I recall, and we were treated or accepted like anyone else. There was never a challenge for a Jewish person entering a particular field or to try for anything where they would be rejected.

I thought this was a nice gesture: I can recall that when I joined the Rotary Club, my father was a member. He wasn't very religious or observant, yet one thing he didn't do is eat ham or bacon. And at the club, being the only Jewish man, they respected him and would make him a special dish every week: When they had ham, they gave him something else. I myself don't participate because I enjoy ham and bacon.

MARCH 5, 1979

❋ 17 ❋

"Nobody Seemed to Give a Damn Who Went to Church"

A. C. BERNSTEIN

A. C. Bernstein was a media and public-relations man whose Hoosier ties ultimately outweighed both his Jewish roots and his show-business connections in determining the course of his career. His ancestors originally came from Alsace-Lorraine and emigrated to the Deep South. His maternal grandfather, Adolf C. Silverburg, was born in Natchez, Mississippi, graduated from the University of Cincinnati Law School, and after graduation worked in the Cincinnati law firm headed by William Howard Taft before moving to Muncie with his brand-new bride, Florence Gregory, a native of Macon, Georgia. When Bernstein was interviewed at his home in Warsaw, in northern Indiana, he was semi-retired, with two daughters, ages twenty-five and twenty-one.

I never knew my father. I think he was born in Farmsdale, Alabama. He graduated from college and somehow got from Alabama to Victoria, Texas. He was in a Catholic orphanage there, and he was adopted by a family named Bernstein—originally *Bearnstein*—I haven't the slightest idea of where the "a" dropped out. He was gassed quite severely in World War I and he had all kinds of medical problems. He did get back to the States, but he died, so I was brought up mainly by my mother and grandmother in Muncie.

My parents met in Muncie, although just what brought my father there—or my mother's family—I never knew. They were married just a few months before he went into the army.

My mother [Minna Silverburg] graduated from Muncie High School [now Muncie Central High School], and she went the best part of the year to a Christian convent in Natchez, Mississippi. From there she had a year at Sophie Newcomb, the women's college at Tulane in New Orleans. She didn't continue because that was her father's wish—he didn't think women needed good educations. He was an excellent corporate lawyer, but I suppose today he'd be considered a real male chauvinist pig. Of course, in my mother's day it was quite something when a girl would get even one year of college. So she stayed home. There was no need to work because my grandfather was loaded. He was the senior partner of a law firm that evolved finally into Silverburg, Bracken & Gray.[1] I was only nine or ten when my grandfather died.

*

I don't think I was aware there was a Jewish community as such in Muncie when I was young. I bummed around with Marty Schwartz when we were kids [in the 1920s], but just because he was a neighbor of mine—not because of the church [i.e., temple] he went to. He lived four or five houses down from me on West Charles Street, but Sparky Walsh and Bud Sample lived in the neighborhood too, and we always bummed around together.

---

[1] The firm's name had further evolved into Defur & Voran at the time of the interview in 1979.

I don't know how religious a man my grandfather [Silverburg] was. I do know that a frequent visitor in our house was a Father Arnold from St. Lawrence [Catholic church], who later became the chief chaplain of the U.S. Army. I cannot recall any processions of rabbis coming to our house. There was one who I guess was a pretty erudite, learned man—Bernard Dorfman. I don't think he lived there; he just came down to conduct services from Lima, Ohio. I think he considered Muncie a vast wasteland because there was no one with the intellectual capacity to challenge him at chess. Whether he was really a good chess player or whether he liked to talk about it, I don't know. I was a little kid then.

My mother was not at all active in the temple. As a little kid I used to go over there once in a while under duress, mainly because my mother told me it would make my grandmother feel better. Actually, I went to mass at St. Lawrence far oftener than I ever did to—what is it, Beth El Temple? Is it still there?

When I was a real little boy, maybe in kindergarten, they had some kind of Sunday school, and we colored pictures of Biblical scenes. Muncie being what it is, with all of their overemphasis on high school basketball, I put purple-and-white uniforms on everyone, and a couple of people got very upset over that. Later on—I'm sure I wasn't yet a teenager—there was a red-haired rabbi. I did nothing but get in fights with him, and I'm sure I was the one who did the provoking. But that's the extent of my Jewish education. I know now about things called *bar mitzvahs*, but I don't think they ever had one.

When I was in high school, it was organized socially with three excellent boys' clubs and two girls' clubs—the equivalent of fraternities and sororities. With my 20/20 hindsight I think it was a lousy situation. But if you didn't belong, oh, you were out. And if you were in a good boys' club you dated girls who belonged to one of the two good girls' clubs. You risked all kinds of being ostracized if you dated a girl out of the pale.

I belonged to something called the Triangle Club; so did Marty Schwartz. I'm not sure what qualified anyone to belong to a club except that they had to get along with the other kids. And looking back on it, the members of all three of the boys' clubs came from families that were extremely well off. And hey—this was during the Depression, but everybody had pretty nice clothes, they took nice summer vacations, and there was quite a bit of money. In those days, unlike today, kids didn't have cars. But came the weekend, you had the family car. The clubs met one night a week, and usually somebody had a car to go to the meeting.

In those days at Christmas, people didn't go to Daytona and Fort Lauderdale to get warm. There was one dance after another for fourteen straight nights. Now, aside from Marty Schwartz, I don't know that any other kids from Jewish families belonged to the Triangle. But it wasn't because Jews were restricted; it was because the few other Jewish boys belonged to other clubs.

I don't think any of us kids gave a thought to who was Jewish and who wasn't. In my own peer group nobody seemed to give a damn who went to church or what church they went to. My friend Sparky Walsh, who obviously isn't Jewish, named his oldest son David for Dave Kallmeyer, whose sister Ann was a good friend of Sparky's. My youngest daughter is Joan Catherine—Joan for Sparky's wife, and Catherine for his daughter. So we all grew up naming our kids for other people that we liked. The only Jewish girl I dated was Peggy Marx, a good-looking gal, but not because she was Jewish—she was convenient. She lived in the neighborhood.

My mother didn't get much out of the Jewish religious community, because for many years before she died she attended the Friends church [in Muncie]—the Society of Quakers. My uncle Shelton Silverburg, who is now dead, was an Episcopalian.

*

I graduated from Muncie High School and went to Kenyon College in Ohio. It was picked for me. My grandmother Silverburg and Mrs. Fred Rose were very dear, old friends. Mr. Rose, I think, was president of the Merchants Trust

Company, now the American National Bank. And they were on several boards together—the Children's Home, the Lawyers' Wives' Club, things like that. All three of the Rose boys went to Kenyon. And my grandmother and my mother decided that little A. C. was going to Kenyon. I kind of leaned toward Lake Forest College, but I was disabused of that quite early.

Incidentally, my two roommates my freshman year at Kenyon—William P. Weeks and Joseph W. Peoples—are both priests in the Episcopal church, and Joe is still a very dear friend of mine. He's in Elk Grove Village, a suburb of Chicago, and we correspond and talk to each other quite frequently.

I was at Kenyon for two and a half years. I dropped out in the mid-part of my junior year because I needed some eye surgery in Muncie. Also, my grandmother had died in 1936, and I got the vibes that my mother kind of liked having me around the house. So I stayed at home and enrolled in Ball State and graduated from there in '42.

I met my wife during my junior year at a Ball State–Butler football game in Indianapolis. She was just a freshman [at Ball State]. She's not Jewish—well, she's from the Irish branch. Her name was Mary Alice Murphy, and she came from the big city of Logansport. One of her two sisters lives on a farm down in Carroll County, near our farm property in the adjacent county Fulton County. Her other sister lives in Fort Wayne.

After the war but before I got out of the service, I had a pretty cushy job in Japan: I was an escort officer for celebrity tours on the USO shows. After I was discharged I got a job in California, handling professional and public relations for a couple of very well-known personalities: Oscar Hammerstein and Richard Rodgers. But I was out of the service a total of two years and ten months before I got one of those recall letters—I had a critical specialty (as a Japanese language officer) and was needed during the Korean War. So they yanked me back in until 1953.

By the time I got out, my California job with Rodgers and Hammerstein had been relocated to New York. I was offered the job back, but my mother was not well and my mother-in-law was getting along in years, so we decided we'd come to Indiana.

Eventually I met Bill Moenhour, who represented the Williams interests in Warsaw—the Warsaw *Times-Union* and the radio station. We got along pretty well, and he offered me the opportunity to come up here. Warsaw wasn't totally unfamiliar to me because it's five minutes from Lake Tippecanoe and Camp Crosley, which is run by the Muncie YMCA, so I'd gone there as a little kid. In fact, in my office I've got a little plaque saying that I received my Junior Red Cross Life-Saving Certificate from Camp Crosley in 1930.

APRIL 27, 1979

❋ 18 ❋

Where the Klan Still Lives

ANN KALLMEYER SECTTOR

*Ann Secttor was born in Muncie in 1920 and spent the first
twenty years of her life there. She was interviewed at her home
in Marion, thirty miles northwest of Muncie, whose mayor, at
the time of the interview, was a local second-generation Jew.
Subsequent to this interview Ann Secttor herself became a
member of Marion's City Council.*

My mother was born in Wabash, Indiana,[1] and my father
came from Detroit. They met in Muncie through mutual relatives. They knew each other three weeks, and then my father
proposed to her and they were married in Wabash. My father
was a traveling salesman, a gambler and a gay blade. He came
to Muncie and set up a clothing store with his brother Herman
Marx. Uncle Herman had come to Muncie to be with the
Ringolds, because his wife's sister was married to Sam Ringold,
and they went into business together before Herman and my

---

[1] A northern Indiana town of 13,000, about fifty miles northwest of
Muncie.

father opened their store. It was "Marx and Kallmeyer" for a while. Then my father and my uncle split and each of them had a store. I was just a small child then. Then my father lost the business and he became a traveling salesman for the Redfern Coat Company out of Toledo, Ohio. He traveled for them for maybe ten or twelve years, until 1933, when he lost the job during the Depression. He became a liquor salesman for Keefer-Stewart out of Indianapolis, until 1936, when he died.

Up until the time my father lost his job we were very well off. After my father died, my mother stayed in Muncie. We had no money; my father left very little insurance. My mother went to work for Bernard Freund's father. I can remember my mother baking goods, and my brother and I used to go out and sell them. I was sixteen, my brother was fourteen, and we finished high school in Muncie. I went to Central Business College in Indianapolis for six months and then came back and finished up in Muncie. My grandmother paid for my schooling at business college. I went to work at the Gas Company, and in 1940 I got married and left. My brother never got to go on to school; he worked in Muncie from the time my father died. When the war broke out he enlisted in the Navy and left Muncie.

*

When I was a girl we always associated with Jewish families, but I never felt any definite Jewishness. There were no other Jewish students in my classes all through school. I knew I was Jewish because I went to Sunday school at a different time than other children. I went to "church" at a different church than the other children went to. I never felt like an outsider, but I knew there was a difference because I knew that Jewish people couldn't get into the country club.

There were other Jews who were younger or older than I was, but no one who was my particular age. We associated in many activities at the temple—suppers, Friday night services, High Holiday services. You must remember that up until I was around twelve years old [1932] it was an affluent community—

a lot of good times, a lot of parties. My father loved to drink, and they used to have big parties there—formal parties with the crystal and the silver and the whole bit.

I know that my father and people of his generation built the temple [in 1922]. My father was one of those people who raised money and built that temple. I don't know how they did it.

I had more non-Jewish friends because I was president of a social club in Muncie. There were many social clubs when I was in high school—Sewing Club, TNC, Violet Club. I was president of TNC for two years. That was the lowest on the scale, economically. The more affluent were in the Sewing Club. My cousin Peggy Marx was the only Jew in the Sewing Club. It was quite a thing that she got in. But the social scene in Muncie was just marvelous. That's why I say the kids today don't have the good times we had. During the Christmas holidays we had a dance every single night. Every night you'd see the girls in a different formal [gown]. I used to work in the gift wrapping department at Ball Stores in Muncie. You'd go to work at nine o'clock in the morning, work 'til nine o'clock at night, go home, change clothes, go to the dance, and next day you were back at work.

My husband-to-be [Julian Secttor] was from Marion,[2] where the social life was much different. They had a bigger Jewish group than we had in Muncie. And the Jewish community used to have dances on New Year's Eve. I came up to Marion for one of those dances with a date from Fort Wayne, and that's where I met Julian. The Jews of Muncie, Anderson, and Marion used to get together for events of that kind. In the late '30s we also had a Jewish youth group in Indiana,[3] but it disintegrated when the war broke out.

---

[2] A city of 40,000—that is, roughly half the size of Muncie—about thirty miles northwest of Muncie.

[3] The Indiana Union of Jewish Youth.

*

I remember my father used to make remarks about people not liking Jews, or "It's because I'm Jewish." And I remember my father taking me down to see a Klan parade in '28 or '29, when I was eight or nine. But it was never [perceived as] a threat.

My parents played a lot of bridge, and they were very social-minded, and they played with non-Jewish couples. But my mother was socially active only in temple affairs—not like I am today in community affairs. Their social life was mostly with the Jewish community, but you must remember they had a larger Jewish community in those days, and the city itself was smaller.

*

Our family always observed the Sabbath. My father gave all the blessings. We lit candles every Friday night and had traditional family meals. We always went to temple every Friday night. On the other hand, we had Christmas trees. As a child, my mother never had a Christmas tree, and she always felt she was missing something.

I was confirmed; I went to Sunday school every week, and I knew that I was different, that I was not a Christian. The [Jewish] values were there; my parents observed them—I think my father had a deeper sense of the meaning than my mother. But my [maternal] grandparents were Christian Scientists, and my grandmother lived with us for a number of years and even took us to the Christian Science church with her occasionally.

[Today] my husband is much more religious than my father ever was. The religion meant more to him; he wanted to raise his children in a particularly religious atmosphere. We've never had a Christmas tree; we've always had Hanukah. My children know the difference [between Hanukah and Christmas] and have been raised that way. They went to temple, though their friends are predominantly gentile. The [Jewish] children that my children were raised with went through Sunday school, they were confirmed, the boys were *bar mitzvah*.

My brother was never *bar mitzvah;* my father didn't think it was necessary. But we were both confirmed.

My children are much more aware of their Jewishness than I ever was. We never celebrated Hanukah in the [public] schools. [This year] we were asked to do it by the teachers, and although my husband and I didn't agree with it, we didn't say no. My children participated in [Christian] religious singing in school, but not Christmas plays.

We are the only Jewish family whose children came back to Marion, besides the mayor, Tony Maidenberg.

My participation in the Jewish community has been much greater in Marion than it ever was in Muncie. Here [in Marion] I really get involved—teaching Sunday school, and being president of the sisterhood, and being on all the boards of the sisterhood. It was just recently that the Jews were allowed in the country club here. Yet this country club was started by the Jews in Marion many years ago. When the Depression came along they couldn't keep up their dues, and then they had to drop it and the Christians took over the club.

Not many Jewish families move to Marion. We have Jewish doctors, we have Jewish people at the mental health clinic, but there are no Jews in industry here. Industry is not bringing them in because we don't have much to offer. The first thing they want to know is: What kind of temple do you have? Who is your rabbi? They don't like the idea of having to commute to Fort Wayne or Indianapolis for what they call a Jewish cultural life. Our rabbis ever since the temple was built have been students from the Hebrew Union College. In fact, the [Marion] temple was built with money from Muncie—from the Ball brothers. Julian's uncle went to them and got a gift to start this temple here in Marion. Now I don't think we've got thirty Jewish families in Marion.

In my own family, my daughter was married to a gentile for eleven years and got a divorce last year. My son was married two years ago to a non-Jew. Jerry's the only one who isn't married; he likes the single life. As I said, my children are the only ones [Jews] who came back to Marion [after college]. They know their position in the community as Jews, yet they have no Jewish friends. So naturally they are integrated into the gentile community.

Julian has had two hip operations in Boston, and one time eight years ago he tried to talk one of the [Boston] Jewish doctors into coming to Marion. But the doctor's wife didn't want to live in a small community; she wanted to live in the city. Now, that may be changing, but it won't change in Marion, Indiana. There's still one Jewish general practitioner here who's been looking for an associate. He wants a Jewish associate and he hasn't been able to find one, and the man is close to seventy.

*

Tony Maidenberg first ran for mayor [of Marion] four years ago. He was a young Jewish person—twenty-eight at that time—who came from an extremely wealthy family, and we expected overtones of anti-Semitism, of the young man's wealth, with his father owning quite a bit of property in the community. But it didn't come out last time.

Now, this time the opponent, Mr. Trebor, the county clerk, said he was working for the little people. I don't know what he means by "little people"—to me, that's an insult. He doesn't want the affluent. He says he doesn't need the business people. He has refused to come to Chamber of Commerce meetings with Tony. Then a few weeks ago the *Chronicle-Tribune,* which is our newspaper, said an investigation of Mr. Trebor's books for '76 and '77 showed they were not so kosher. And the politics started to get a little dirty.

On the morning of Good Friday—this is a little ironic; whether they picked that morning purposely or not, we'll never know—a cross was burned at the home of Jake Weinberg, one of our Jewish citizens. He is a widower who has been involved in Marion politics a long time. He was a good friend of Mr. Trebor's. Jake was blamed as the source where the newspaper got its information. We'll never know whether it was a Klan person that burned that cross, because our county has the second-largest Klan registration in the state of Indiana. There are also many, many sympathizers who are not registered Klansmen. Fisher Body [auto plant] is full of them. Constantly we hear that they have propaganda right on their [plant] bulletin boards. The blacks are most concerned about this. We have a large Catholic community; they are much concerned about this. But I'm more aware of it because I have worked on the Human Rights Commission, I've worked with the Police Department. Anybody can go down and see that list of Klan members. But the business people in this community are kind of pushing us aside, and until something like this comes up they don't want to think about it.

The cross-burning received a lot of coverage—pictures showing Jake and the burning cross. It was five foot high and four foot wide and covered with soaked burlap.

You know, it was a Jewish person who saw the fire. Dick Simon's daughter woke him up and they tried to rouse Jake, but they couldn't get him up. He slept through the whole thing. He didn't know about it until the next morning, when Tony called and told him.

The only time we were accepted socially [in Marion] was in organizational work. The whole community has served on United Way organizations. For organizational work we're very acceptable. Socially we were not so terribly accepted. We had been at the country club for civic affairs, but Jewish couples were turned down for membership. About ten years ago we [Jews] got together as a community and refused to go to anything [at the club] until they opened it up, and they finally opened it up. And now most of us are in it. Now we're working on the blacks.

APRIL 27, 1979

❊19❊

The Great Transformation

SHERMAN ZEIGLER

Sherman Zeigler was an active member of numerous civic and business boards in Muncie, as well as a supporter of Ball State University. Although he strongly identified himself as a Jew, and his parents contributed to a fund that brought Jewish speakers and cultural figures to the campus, neither he nor his parents belonged to the temple in Muncie.

My father arrived here when he was twenty-four, and one of the basic purposes of his leaving Lithuania, which was then under Russian rule, was to escape being drafted into the Russian army. He had an uncle in the scrap business in Anderson, Indiana,[1] and he financed my father's trip to this country and to Anderson. The uncle's purpose was partly to gather the family together but also because, in those days before the country was so highly industrialized, the basis of a successful scrap business was to have satellites with a horse and wagon going through the countryside, buying scrap, bringing it to a central

---

[1] A city of 50,000 about twenty miles southwest of Muncie.

location, and shipping it from the central location to Anderson, where it was prepared and then sold and shipped to the steel mills.

My father was financed with a horse and wagon and toured the area around Osgood as far as Versailles [in southern Indiana]. He couldn't go into Versailles because a horse with a loaded wagon couldn't pull the hills. So they had to stay out of areas that were too hilly, but they operated in that part of southern Indiana, buying scrap from farmers—not only scrap iron, but rubber, which was really in demand, furs, bones for fertilizer, glass, all this type of thing.

My father had a brother Max—also brought to Anderson with the same uncle—whom he peddled with on the horse and wagon. In many cases they didn't get on too well. So they parted company, and the brother came to Muncie, which at that time had one scrap dealer. After being here for a short time, the brother again approached my father and told him that things would be different, that it was a great opportunity in Muncie, and wouldn't he come in with him? This my father did, but after a short time together they again parted company. My father established his own business in 1916.

My father spoke no English when he came here, but he did learn, and he developed a great vocabulary. He never did learn the fine points of American grammar—he never perfected that—but he had a fantastic use of words. He attended night school for a while in Indianapolis, which is where he was actually trained in basic English.

I was born in Muncie in 1921, on what is now the Ball State [University] campus. My family never owned a car—neither of my parents learned to drive—but growing up just across from the main campus building was an experience in itself. There was always excitement. The Ball State homecoming at that time, the football games, were great experiences. Instead of going in through the gate, naturally we went in over the fence.

As I grew a little older, the girls were interesting to watch, too. The students and the faculty were always friendly and fun to be with. I lived next door to a restaurant called the Pine Shelf, which was where some of the bootleg hootch was consumed by Ball State students—this at a time when there wasn't even smoking allowed on Ball State's campus. Here we watched some of the lovemaking that took place among the Ball State students. It was just an exciting time and location to grow up in.

*

I was never confirmed, I never had my *bar mitzvah*, I never had a religious education as far as the temple was concerned. But my dad was very religious philosophically. In fact, in the old country my dad had studied to be a rabbi but had rebelled against it as a young man. He never belonged to the temple here, and neither have I. But he was very learned in Jewish history, Jewish religion, Jewish background. And of course as I grew up a lot of this was passed on to me. My moral values are based on the religion, which really isn't all that different from any other religion.

I worked summers in the scrap yard from the time I was twelve years old. I graduated from Burris [High] School and entered the Navy. As a line officer I was sent to Berea College in Kentucky. Then the Navy wanted me to become a supply officer, so I could use to good effect what experience I had in the scrap business. So I was sent to the University of North Carolina, and that's where I received my education.

After being in practically every part of the U.S. during World War II, I came back to Muncie when the war ended. It was a basic decision I had to make. I had enjoyed the scrap business; it always fascinated me; and I decided Muncie was the right size town. I felt I had a future in the scrap business, and that the scrap business had a future in Muncie. And my parents lived here.

Most of the Jews in Muncie then were in business. I don't recall any Jewish teachers or professors. I know that as I grew up as a boy it was even difficult for a Jew to get a job in an industrial plant: If a non-Jew's application was there, the Jew was passed over. The Jews mainly had small clothing stores; the Greeks had the candy and grocery stores. I think there was one Jewish lawyer here at the time.

In my earliest years the Jews led a very restricted social life—mostly with other Jews. Oh, my father was invited to join the United Fund and their plan meetings for fund collections; he was invited to the yearly Chamber of Commerce meetings. But as far as social associations, he couldn't belong to the country club, he couldn't belong to the Muncie Club, he couldn't belong to the Elks. I think one or two Jews belonged to the Moose. But most of the social and civic clubs were closed to the Jews.

In my father's generation there were not many Jews involved in the community's life. This was not by choice, but it didn't really affect the Jew as deeply as you'd think, because he was busy "making it." He was working twelve, fifteen hours a day so that his kids could get a college education. This was, next to health, the most important thing. It was important that the children get a college education at a good, well-accepted school so they could rise above the opportunities that their parents had.

At Burris School, fortunately for me, there were mostly upper-class and upper-middle-class children. They were well-mannered, by and large. Though there were no doubt anti-Semitic feelings among them and their families, they were polite. I was always indebted to Burris School, because of the consideration that the teachers showed to me and my youngest sister—the respect that they gave my family and the good feeling of the kids there. I was always thankful that I lived in "Normal City" and that that's where I went to school.

Rarely was there confrontation. Oh, I can remember two or three that did take place. I remember one bully who used to chase me home and rough me up pretty good, tear up my clothes. He'd call me a damn Jew and a Christ-killer. I'd go home crying, and I'd ask my mother why he did this. She told me, "He knows you're better than he is, and he's just jealous."

Well, as I grew up I realized that some day I'd be married and have a family, and if this ever happened to my kids, what could I tell them? I always wondered. When my mother told me that, I knew it wasn't so—she just told me that to make me feel good.

I married, had two boys and lived in practically the same neighborhood that I grew up in. As my boys grew up they experienced the give-and-take that kids have in school, and my kids were always aware of their Jewish father (although their mother wasn't Jewish). They were always aware of his feeling toward Judaism—not a religious Judaism but a philosophical one—and they never came home roughed up. They never came home and told their dad that fellows called them "damn Jews." Why?

And one evening it was supper time and the boys—then eleven and thirteen—hadn't returned. They came in late, washed up, and sat down at the table. We asked them where they were.

"Well," they said, "we were at the bridge."

I said, "What do you mean?" They said they were in a challenge at the bridge. I said, "What kind of challenge at the bridge?" They said Perry Cross's son had challenged another boy at the bridge because he had insulted his aunt, and they stayed to see the fight.

So here was my opportunity. I said, "Have fellows ever picked on you and called you damn Jews, called you Christ-killers?" And both of them laughed. Of course I resented that they laughed, because this was a very serious subject with me. I said, "What are you laughing about?" Their reaction, aside from the laughter, was, "Why should they do *that?*" It was completely foreign; they hadn't heard it and they couldn't imagine me asking a question like that.

Now, I realize that's pretty simplified, and it [anti-Semitism] probably happens in our neighborhood. But it amazed me that our boys had not run into this in the same normal city that I used to get roughed up in.

To me it shows you the change in attitude and in the thinking of the country. As a result of the war, when many soldiers
went all over the world, we aren't as insulated as we once were.
The servicemen saw many religions and nationalities, and so
the differences didn't make that much difference to them.

*

When I was twelve years old, a friend and I applied to
the Muncie *Press* circulation department for a paper route.
There was a route open in my neighborhood, and they said
they'd let us know in a few days. Of course I was super-anx-
ious, twelve years old and eager to earn my own money carrying papers. At that age it seemed to me to be a thrilling
occupation. I didn't hear from them, but I ran into the young
man I had applied with. When I asked if he had heard from
them, he said yes.

"What did they say?"

"Well," he said, "I got the route."

I said, "I never heard from them. Am I going to get it? Did
they say anything about me?"

I could tell by the way he acted that he had something he
wanted to tell me. "Bob," I told him, "be honest with me. Am
I going to get this job?"

He said, "If you promise not to say anything about it, I'll
tell you." I promised. He said, "You're not going to get it." I
asked why, but I already suspected why. "Because they didn't
want any Jews working on their paper," he said.

It came as quite a shock. I was heartbroken, and I went
home and told my father about it, and I could tell he was heartbroken too, because he didn't want to see that happen to his
children.

I didn't say anything about it. But about three days later,
the newspaper's circulation manager plus the publisher
called and asked if they could talk with my father and myself. They came out to the house and said there had been a
misunderstanding. The publisher said that he was Catholic
himself and would never think of restricting anyone because

of religion, and he apologized. The circulation manager said that he had been misunderstood, and that if I still wanted the job, it was mine.

What I didn't know was that my father had told this to several of his Jewish friends who had stores on Walnut Street. At that time the Muncie *Star* and the *Evening Press* were separate companies, and when the *Press* solicited these merchants for their ads, they said, "If you don't give Jews jobs, we don't give you ads." So it was an economic thing, and they did come and offered me the job on a platter.

My parents didn't want me to take the job because of their pride, but I wanted it so bad that I took it. Incidentally, I increased my route by more new customers than any other carrier.

*

A couple of years after I'd come back from the service, my wife and I picked out a house. We'd been looking in magazines that showed different plans of homes, and we picked out a house that we wanted. In riding around the area we picked out a lot with trees where we thought this house would fit in perfectly. We knew there were restrictions in Westwood and Kenmore; I was just starting in business; my wife at that time worked as a legal secretary in a law firm here; and we certainly didn't want to offend anybody or rock the boat.

We found a lot in Mann Addition, which was just opposite Westwood. The real estate broker for this lot was a fellow named Swain. Before agreeing to purchase the lot, I asked Mr. Swain—an old-time Muncie real estate man who was really a very nice person—"Is this area restricted?" I specifically said we didn't want to offend anyone or create a hassle, but we didn't want to go ahead and make plans if the area was restricted.

He said, "I anticipated that question and I went ahead and made inquiry of the gentleman who platted the addition"—a man named Tom Mann. "And he said the only restriction is that you be good neighbors, both you and your wife, and he saw no reason why you couldn't build there." So we made the down payment on the lot and purchased it.

Well, about two days after that, a non-Jewish friend of my father's said to him, "Ben, I was in the bank this morning, and your son isn't making friends in the community." My dad said, "How is that?" He said, "Well, he bought a lot in a restricted addition and is going to build a home."

My father told me this, and he was really very emotional about it when he told me this. I told him there must be a mistake, because we did make inquiry. "Let me double-check," I said. So I went to Swain, the real estate man, and told him what had happened.

"I can't understand that," Swain said. "When I made the original inquiry, they told me the only restriction was that you be good neighbors. But now it's also bled back to me that it *is* restricted."

I told him, "Well, Mr. Swain, I could make an issue of it, but I don't choose to, because I certainly don't want to live where I'm not wanted. But I would like my down payment back."

"You certainly will get it," he said.

I waited thirty days and didn't receive the down payment. I waited sixty days and didn't receive the down payment. I contacted Mr. Swain again and asked him about it. "Please give me a little longer," he said. "When you made that down payment, I invested it in another project, and I haven't been able to retrieve it yet. But be patient."

I decided that if I didn't get it back in another fifteen days I would go to my wife's law firm, which was one of the firms that was very influential in enforcing the restrictions on the plats in this addition. When I didn't receive the check within fifteen days, I went up to see one of the firm's leading attorneys and told him I'd like to file suit. He said, "Certainly. I don't blame you a bit. We'll institute suit immediately." The next day I had a check in full for the down payment.

*

Many people who belonged to the Klan [in the 1920s] would deal only with other Klan members, so there was some financial effect on families like ours. But at that time the Klan excluded Catholics as well as Jews, and there were quite a large group of Catholic businessmen in the community, and they sort of cleaved together. For instance, there were Catholic automobile wreckers in town whom my father bought scrap from who would only sell their scrap to a Jew. So the boycott the Klan tried to implement wasn't as effective as you'd expect had there been no Catholics in the community.

*

Many of the sons and daughters of Jewish families who leave Muncie for their education settle elsewhere because the opportunity is greater. But as opportunities for professionals develop in Muncie, I feel there are Jews who will come to Muncie, that the youth will come back.

I have two sons, neither one of whom is interested in the scrap business. The second would be ideal, not only as a businessman but in the industrial scrap business. But he graduates from Brown University this June and he wishes not to come back to Muncie and not to go into business. At this point he wants to get into social work. He wants to save the world. Maybe that's part of the philosophical Judaism that he got at home. But frankly, I feel that he's carrying it a bit too far. However, the choice is his. All I ask is that he be a good citizen, a good American, be decent.

*

I grew up in a very prejudiced and anti-Semitic community. In fact, Muncie was even more anti-Semitic than Anderson, Logansport, Fort Wayne. A few of the Jews in Anderson and Fort Wayne could belong to the civic clubs; the Jews were restricted from the civic clubs here. Of course, as a young man it didn't mean anything to me, but I knew that situation existed. We were restricted from the country club, so they [the Jews] developed their own, which never flew, and which I don't believe they really enjoyed that much. We were certainly restricted in job opportunities. This is one of the reasons there were so many Jewish businessmen at that time—because if you weren't hired, you created your own opportunities.

But since I came back from the service, that attitude—I don't know whether it's gone underground or whether it's completely changed. My observation is that it's changed, it's a different atmosphere altogether. We're now in the civic clubs of our choice, we're accepted in the country club, we're accepted in the Elks, which we hadn't been. We're accepted in the Muncie Club. We have complete social equality, where after World War II we had no social equality.

I'm not naive enough to think that anti-Semitism doesn't still exist. There are still many Jew-haters in the community. But it's a different atmosphere, a different culture altogether. I think we Jews feel unburdened, I think we respect our fellow non-Jews, and I think we're respected by them. Maybe it's a little too much to ask to be loved by them. But as long as we have their respect and as long as we have justice, why, that's all we can ask for.

*

My father was always a very ardent Zionist. I heard Zionism as I grew up. It wasn't preached to me, but my father was a very ardent reader. He almost worshipped books. One of his specialties were books on Zionism, so that was part of my background. I myself am a Zionist. I'm not ardent, but I contribute to the cause. I think it's important for the preservation of Jewish culture. Probably subconsciously I feel, as most other Jews feel, that in case we should see a repeat performance of the Germany situation here, we'd have a place to run.

Keep in mind that the Jew in [pre-Hitler] Germany was the most assimilated Jew in all of Europe. Probably 40 percent of German Jewish marriages at that time were to non-Jews. Yet when the boom fell on the Jews, it fell hardest there of any place in the world. And even though in the United States we have arrived at what is really the golden age—the opportunity and acceptance is unequaled—because of this history the insecurity lurks in the back of the Jew's mind, and subconsciously you always wonder when you're going to need that open door.

*

I have not regretted my choice in coming back to Muncie. To be perfectly honest with you, I'm very proud of Muncie. I'm very proud of the changes that have been made in Muncie. I'm very proud of the acceptance of all minorities that I've seen develop in Muncie. I really feel that Muncie is as fine a place to live as a Jew and as an American as any place in the entire continent.

FEBRUARY 26, 1979

EPILOGUE

Of the nineteen Muncie Jews interviewed for this project in 1979, ten still survived when this book went to press in 1996. Allen Burgauer, Bernard Freund, Beulah Lazar, Bud Roth, and Martin Schwartz remained in Muncie; Ann Secttor still lived in Marion; Pearl Shonfield and Bob Burgauer in Indianapolis; and Rachel Lipp in Fort Wayne. Joe Freadlin maintained his home in Winchester but increasingly spent most of his time in Florida.

Ben Hertz's business, Midwest Towel, was sold before his death to a large company based in Missouri. Martin Schwartz, having failed to interest any of his four daughters in returning to Muncie to take over the family business, sold the Schwartz Paper Company in 1990 to a local competitor. Prior to Sherman Zeigler's death in 1987, he sold his family's scrap metal concern, the Ben Zeigler Company, to Dobrow Industries, which is now owned by Sam Dobrow's son Ed.

By 1996 the Jewish retailing presence had vanished altogether from Muncie. Pazol Jewelers, the last Jewish store on Walnut Street, still functioned but was no longer family owned, having been sold by Mort and Herb Pazol in the mid–1980s, before Mort's death.

To the extent that new Jewish faces were attracted to Muncie in 1996, the prime magnets attracting them were not so much business opportunities as academic and professional opportunities at Ball State University (which had been a state teachers' college until 1965) and Ball Memorial Hospital. The size of the Jewish community remained stagnant at roughly two hundred, but that number included many Jews who downplayed their Jewish identity and/or were unaffiliated with Temple Beth El. The community lacked a strong central core of Jewishness aside from a small nucleus of committed families. The B'nai B'rith chapter existed in name only. In an age of career women, the temple sisterhood was a shadow organization that rarely met and even lacked formal officers. The Temple itself continued to function, albeit without a regular rabbi.

D. R.

AFTERWORD

Martin D. Schwartz

Jewish history tells of turmoil, tragedy, and redemption. The twentieth century has been painfully marked by the first two. The story of American Jews is about the third element, also a significant fact of the century, which has seen a relatively small American Jewish population in the nineteenth century increase exponentially from waves of principally eastern European immigrants.

These immigrants and their progeny found homes and productive lives in large urban areas, but they also moved into smaller cities and towns throughout the country. Where they prospered economically they became rooted, and were integrated into these communities—so far as they were permitted. Hostility and prejudice were their only barriers.

Their first-generation children grew up primarily as Americans and sometimes only incidentally as Jews. Many left the smaller communities where their families were settled and moved to larger, more attractive places where opportunity appeared more abundant. In many of these small towns there are no longer Jewish communities. In others, there is still a viable Jewish presence. Middletown, *a.k.a.* Muncie, Indiana, is one of those.

Previous chapters of this book reflect a Muncie Jewish community of mostly small merchants with an occasional attorney. Jewish physicians were rare and never part of the congregation. Now, the community is comprised mostly of Ball State University faculty, a few professional men and women, and an even smaller group of business people and retirees. The purpose of this book is to preserve a sense of the community that existed from the 1920s through the 1960s.

Oral history, like a documentary film, is a way of recording events in people's lives. But since memory is selective, the observations recounted are significant as much for what they don't say as for what they do. Some of these stories happened after World War I. Some are first-person recollections, others are repeated from hearsay. Nevertheless, there is a common theme throughout: the Ku Klux Klan, anti-Semitism, and, in general, exclusion from the mainstream of the society in which these Jews lived.

To talk about the Jewish community during this period is somewhat misleading. There were Jews who lived in Muncie for part or most of their lives, but they hardly constituted a monolithic community. Their great diversity in background created internal tensions within the group that were exacerbated by the marginality of their existence in the larger society. That was not unique for Jews in small-town America. But it was particularly noticeable for Muncie Jews, who were sensitized by restrictive housing covenants, the exclusionary agenda of the business and social establishment, and the limited interchange between Jews and gentiles. World War II initiated a more open society. Today there is only a dim awareness in the Muncie Jewish community of those limitations and legacies. Historical memory is short.

The stories told here are vignettes of people's lives. They emphasize, among other things, the duality of the Jewish experience, i.e., that Judaism is both a religion and an ethnic identity or peoplehood. To the outside world, this distinction is seldom noted because Jews are generally considered members of both a religion and an identifiable ethnic group. The term or epithet *race* is sometimes used, but is hardly a scientific description. Jews share a long history of being different from the host communities in which they lived—whether Christian or Islamic—by virtue of their customs, traditions, and beliefs.

Religion was always the identifying and differentiating factor in lands where Jews resided, and they were accustomed to community structures that were hierarchical, both politically and religiously.

Jewish experience in the United States is quite different from that in other lands because the unique separation of church and state made religious identity less distinguishing. Like other Americans, Jews embraced wholeheartedly the idea of a secular society distinct from one based on religious authority.

In these reminiscences, there is little reference to Jewish religious needs or practices. A few families always kept the dietary laws, but that was not a major concern for most. A Jew or a gentile married to one (a relatively uncommon event in those days) recognized that there were areas closed to him or her because of that identity. However, when economic needs were being met, most Jews stayed to earn a living in Muncie. If such needs were not satisfied, they left.

The Temple was dedicated in 1922, but the organized Jewish congregation that centered around the Temple was not the religious home of all Muncie Jews. Seventy-five years later, it is still not part of the life of every Jew in Muncie. The very word *Temple* as a place of worship is a creation of the Reform Jewish movement, and refers to the Jewish heritage dating from the original Temple in Jerusalem. Now, many Jews comfortably call it a synagogue, which it is, but that terminology commonly referred to Orthodox Jewish places of worship. Much of the tension endemic in the group results from the attempt by Jews from more Orthodox or traditional origins to adjust to a Reform Jewish congregation much less rigorous in religious observance. As there is no other Jewish place of worship in Muncie, the Beth El congregation adapted for its members a broad spectrum of Jewish religious practices, from interpretations of Orthodoxy to a minimum of perfunctory Jewish rituals. There were always Jews in Muncie (and still are) who never affiliated with the congregation or who did so only sporadically. This fact is puzzling to non-Jews, who assume that all

Jews are in sync with each other spiritually and emotionally. There is no ultimate religious authority over all American Jews. Most congregations follow a democratic process of selecting their own lay leaders, rabbis, and ritual observances.

This small Temple, home to the congregation, is the single public and tangible symbol of a Jewish presence in Muncie. It is an architectural gem typical of the style built in the first third of the century and has been carefully preserved and maintained.

Muncie Jews are still divided at the end of the twentieth century, just as they were in the 1920s, but now those divisions are more ideological than social. At issue is the very survival of the Jewish people and Judaism itself in the United States. Some think this can only be realized by a welcoming, inclusive effort to bring all family members of a Jewish spouse into the synagogue. Others argue that only more Jewish exclusivity, education, and religious practices will guarantee the future of Judaism. The possibility of Judaism's demise through intermarriage and gradual secularization concerns most thoughtful Jews. What they don't agree on is how to counter those trends.

During a four-thousand-year history the Jewish people have survived Egyptian slavery, Babylonian captivity, Roman dispersion, the Crusades, the Inquisition, the Holocaust, and more. Jews adapted to the realities of their times and the places where they were permitted to exist, sometimes with only bare-bones knowledge of their covenant with God that determined their identity and therefore their fate.

Even today the power and mystique of the covenant binds Jews with ties or traditions that often seem to unravel but still remain intact.

SEPTEMBER 1996

BIBLIOGRAPHY

BOOKS

Caplow, Theodore, et al. *All Faithful People*. Minneapolis, 1983.

Emerson's Muncie Directory. Indianapolis, Ind., 1891 ff.

Endelman, Judith B. *The Jewish Community of Indianapolis, 1849 to the Present*. Bloomington, Ind., 1984.

Gordon, Whitney H. *A Community in Stress*. New York: Living Books, 1964.

Haimbaugh, Frank D., ed. *History of Delaware County, Indiana*. Two vols., Indianapolis, 1924.

Helm, Thomas B. *History of Delaware County, Indiana*. Chicago, 1881.

Jackson, Kenneth T. *The Ku Klux Klan in the City, 1915–1930*. New York, 1967.

Lipman, Eugene J., and Albert Vorspan. *A Tale of Ten Cities: The Triple Ghetto in American Religious Life*. New York: Union of American Hebrew Congregations, 1964.

Lynd, Robert S., and Helen M. Lynd. *Middletown: A Study in Contemporary American Culture*. New York: Harcourt, Brace & Co., 1929.

———. *Middletown in Transition*. New York: Harcourt, Brace & Co., 1937.

Madison, James H. *Indiana through Tradition and Change: A History of the Hoosier State and Its People, 1920–1945*. Indianapolis, Ind., 1982.

Manufacturing and Mercantile Resources and Industries of the Principal Places of Indiana, Wayne, Henry, Delaware, and Randolph Counties. 1881.

Raphael, Marc Lee. *Jews and Judaism in a Midwestern Community: Columbus, Ohio, 1840–1875*. Columbus, Ohio, 1979.

Shonfield, Alexander L. *Preface to the History of the Jewish People and a Sketch of Muncie, Indiana*. Fort Wayne, Ind., 1977.

ARTICLES AND PAPERS

Bracken, Alexander E. "Muncie as a Pioneer Community." Ph.D. dissertation, Department of History, Ball State University, Muncie, Indiana, 1978.

Frank, Carrolyle M. "Politics in Middletown: A Reconsideration of Municipal Government and Community Power in Muncie, Indiana, 1925–1935." Ph.D. dissertation, Department of History, Ball State University, Muncie, Indiana, 1974.

Harvey, Charles E. "Robert S. Lynd, John D. Rockefeller, Jr., and *Middletown.*" *Indiana Magazine of History* LXXIX (December 1983), 330–54. See also *Journal of the History of Sociology,* Vol. 2 (Fall-Winter 1979–80), issue devoted to Robert S. Lynd.

Morris, Judith. "A Focal Study of the Bernard Freund Family." Seminar paper, Ball State University, Muncie, Indiana, November 1980.

Thernstrom, Stephan. "Reflections on the New Urban History." *Daedalus* C (Spring 1971), 366.

Toll, William. "The Chosen People in the World of Choice." *Reviews in American History* VIII (June 1980).

DAN ROTTENBERG

is the author of six books on diverse subjects, including *Finding Our Fathers,* the first English-language guide to tracing Jewish ancestors. Following his graduation from the University of Pennsylvania in 1964, he spent four years with the Portland (Ind.) *Commercial-Review,* located thirty miles northeast of Muncie. The friendships he developed at that time led, more than a quarter century later, to his involvement in the Muncie Jews oral history project and his editing of this book. He is presently editor of the *Philadelphia Forum,* a weekly Philadelphia opinion paper which he founded in 1996, as well as an editorial-page columnist for the *Philadelphia Inquirer.*